P9-EJP-696

Carnevale Italiano

Also by the authors:

THE ROMAGNOLIS' TABLE
THE NEW ITALIAN COOKING

Carnevale Italiano

THE ROMAGNOLIS' MEATLESS COOKBOOK

Margaret and G. Franco Romagnoli

Photographs by G. Franco Romagnoli

An Atlantic Monthly Press Book

Little, Brown and Company   Boston   Toronto

COPYRIGHT © 1976 BY MARGARET ROMAGNOLI AND
G. FRANCO ROMAGNOLI

ALL RIGHTS RESERVED. NO PART OF THIS BOOK MAY BE REPRO-
DUCED IN ANY FORM OR BY ANY ELECTRONIC OR MECHANICAL
MEANS INCLUDING INFORMATION STORAGE AND RETRIEVAL SYS-
TEMS WITHOUT PERMISSION IN WRITING FROM THE PUBLISHER,
EXCEPT BY A REVIEWER WHO MAY QUOTE BRIEF PASSAGES IN
A REVIEW.

Originally published as *The Romagnolis' Meatless Cookbook.*

LIBRARY OF CONGRESS CATALOGING IN PUBLICATION DATA

Romagnoli, Margaret.
The Romagnolis' Meatless cookbook.
"An Atlantic Monthly Press book."
Includes index.
1.   Lenten menus.   2.   Cookery, Italian.   I.   Romagnoli,
G. Franco, joint author.   II.   Title.
III.   Title: Meatless cookbook.
TX837.R77   641.5'66'0945   76-11838
ISBN 0-316-75564-8

ATLANTIC–LITTLE, BROWN BOOKS
ARE PUBLISHED BY
LITTLE, BROWN AND COMPANY
IN ASSOCIATION WITH
THE ATLANTIC MONTHLY PRESS

MV

*Published simultaneously in Canada
by Little, Brown & Company (Canada) Limited*

PRINTED IN THE UNITED STATES OF AMERICA

To Jean and Robert and Rita and Italo, who at our various tables have shared our wild, hilarious schemes for a simpler, eminently livable life.

INTRODUCTION

While the word *carnevale* conjures visions of masquerades, revelry, ribald merrymaking, and the pleasures of the flesh in general, ironically the origin of the word comes directly from the Latin. *Carne* (meat or flesh) and *levare* (to take away, lift up) mean doing away with meat, or "here we go, meatless." Hence the title of this book.

Among all these divisions of Italian cooking, it would be unfair not to include a subdivision common to them all. It is called *cucina di magro*. The adjective *magro* means thin, lean, spare, as in *le sette vacche magre*, the seven lean kine. It is the opposite of *grasso*, fat, as in *il Grassone e il Magrolino*, the Italian nicknames for Oliver Hardy and Stan Laurel. The *cucina di magro* could then be translated as "thin cookery," but "meatless kitchen" is more accurate since it excludes from its ingredients all meats. *Cucina di magro* is not vegetarian cooking, because it leaves the kitchen door open to fish.

Just as traditional a style as all the others in the Italian peninsula, it dates officially from around the fourth century, the time when the Roman Catholic Church made fasting and abstinence from meat one of its precepts, a rule to be obeyed during the forty days of Lent, the twenty-five of Advent, every Friday of the year, and on the many *giorni di vigilia,* the days preceding major religious holidays. All told, nearly one-third of the year was devoted to *cucina di magro*. Until recently, believers followed the precept scrupulously: breaking it was a venial sin. On the other hand, a few things helped to soften the minor sacrifice. For the more affluent urban populace there was the anticipation of making up for it the next feast day. As for the hard-pressed rural population, meat days were already, by and large, exceptions to a diet that was of necessity mostly vegetarian. Furthermore, the Italian love of a good meal combined with the equally characteristic native ingenuity in making the best of any given situation produced a very rewarding variety of meatless dishes, and perhaps saved a little money to boot.

A few years ago the religious rule was abolished and abstinence made voluntary. This should have diminished the importance of the *cucina di magro,* but the meatless meal is still very much a part of the weekly menu. The reasons for its persisting vitality are many: firmly established family tastes and habits; the belief that if meat is good for you, too much of it is not; a dedication to a vegetarian regime for definite health reasons, as when animal fats in the diet must be reduced. Throughout Italy people have always had great faith in the medicinal power of many vegetables and herbs. Doctors and mothers alike recommend a light vegetable diet to filter out impurities in the blood (*disintossicare il sangue*), as a valid cure for acne, for high blood pressure, and for all post-*festa* ailments. Yet taste was not sacrificed in such a diet. Special attention, in fact, was given to make the "medicinal" diet more attractive.

Strict vegetarians will not allow fish in their diet, although it certainly has its place in *cucina di magro.* Why fish was permitted on days of abstinence can be explained by the highly symbolic value it had in the early Catholic Church. It came to represent nourishment for the soul, and, after all, if St. Peter was a fisherman, fish couldn't be all that bad.

Fish on the vigil day table has had good company: at one time frogs, beavers, ducks, and young rabbits were allowed. Since this concession was taken too liberally by certain clergy who became more rubicund with each passing day of Lent, these other creatures were struck from the diet.

"Fish on Friday" came to be understood by the majority of

the people as a sort of obligation. No doubt the belief was encouraged by the fishmongers for whom Friday was the best selling day and who, fearing a slackening in the consumption of fish, showed a good deal of resentment and even, it is said, threatened to strike against the abolition of the vigil-day rule.

There are also meatless dishes in which fish, mostly salted anchovies, appears in such small quantities that it becomes an accent, much as an herb or spice. The use of fish in this manner can be traced back to pre-Christian Roman times, when *liquamen*, a sauce made of salted, fermented fish, was used to accompany all sorts of dishes. This accent can be eliminated at the cook's discretion without terrible damage to the dish. To be true to tradition, we have included recipes that use fish both as an ingredient and as an accent, but we have grouped them together for convenience.

Italy's geography, topography, and climate, which goes from temperate to subtropical, are exceptionally encouraging to the growth of a large variety of native vegetables. Many imported species (such as the South American tomato and potato, the Southeast Asian eggplant) have prospered on Italian soil. Another advantage for the Italian cook is the relatively small size of the country: vegetables, no matter in which region grown, have a short way to go from field to market, and reach the table at their best. Hence he prefers to follow the seasons and make the most of their offerings. Nearly all vegetables used in Italian cooking are readily available on the American market, but some, unfortunately, have to travel quite a distance, and reach the consumer when they are slightly past their prime. Some, for marketing reasons, are ripened in the box, not on the plant, with a resultant loss in texture and flavor. Under normal conditions we gladly use the markets' offerings, but for an even better selection, we seek out local fresh vegetable stalls and take our pick.

Since the whole idea of *cucina di magro* is one of discreet penance — giving up for Lent, as it were — the organization of a meal should theoretically be austere, doing away with such frills as *antipasto* and dessert. It should provide just nourishment, a sober, balanced diet achieved through a first course (a *primo piatto* of pasta, rice, or soup); a second course (*secondo piatto* of hearty vegetable dishes or fish or eggs); plus a *contorno,* a side dish. The traditional dessert was just fruit.

But today the *cucina di magro* has lost most of its penitential character, and since so many people enjoy a meatless meal, its modified format tends to include *antipasto* (something to munch on and to tease the appetite) before the first course, and a *dolce,* or sweet, at the end of the meal.

Strangely enough, the *cucina di magro* instead of restricting the composition of a meal seems to permit more flexibility than one would think. Many meatless dishes can appear and hold their own either as *antipasti, secondi,* or *contorni,* which cannot be said for their meat counterparts.

The choice of the various dishes that compose a menu is governed by a few basic rules of common sense and, naturally, by personal taste. Not only should the dishes strive for a balance of nutritional value but they should also complement each other in taste, texture, and, where possible, color. The order of their appearance on the table should be one in which — in the best operatic fashion — each dish stands on its own performance and also prepares for the appearance of the next. As in grand opera, where the difference in pitch between an alto and a basso is used to mutual advantage, the contrasting tastes of dishes in a menu should be played so that they enhance rather than fight each other. Not to abandon the theatrical metaphor, at the end of a well-orchestrated meal, no matter how simple or rich, you and your guests should stand up and say: "Ah, that was a performance! Encore!"

CONTENTS

Illustrations

A WORD
ABOUT BASICS

In MEATLESS COOKING, some basic ingredients and sauces tend to cross the boundaries between categories and appear with justification in either *antipasti,* first or second courses, or *contorni,* side dishes. To make things easier we'll discuss here these common elements in general terms. We may give advice, describe techniques, or even give full recipes.

VERDURE / VEGETABLES

ARTICHOKES are a vegetable prepared in a great variety of ways in Italy. They show up in the spring in the United States and are usually about the size of that other spring phenomenon, the baseball. Their size is only one aspect, however. Big or small, they must be firm and tightly closed, not unlike a rosebud, in order to have the proper taste and texture. The more open the leaves, the more fibrous and woody they are and the less edible. Artichokes are generally sold individually rather than by the pound, so a small but firmly closed one is a better buy than a large, open-leafed one. To prepare artichokes, tear off the tough outer leaves

Choose firm artichokes whose leaves are tightly closed. Before cooking, some leaves will be discarded, as well as the inedible thistlelike center, the choke. Cut artichokes should be rubbed with lemon to prevent discoloration.

To prepare, tear off the tough fibrous outer leaves until they snap as they are torn, revealing the pale green tender ones. Have the courage to discard *all* the tough leaves.

With a very sharp paring knife, trim the remaining part of the outer leaves and the fibrous outside of the stem.

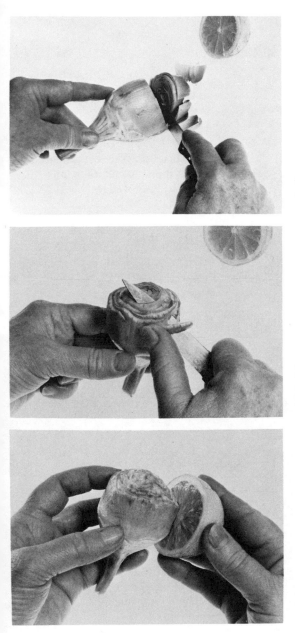

Cut off about ⅓ of the top of the artichoke.

Pare around the artichoke to cut off any remaining inedible and fibrous part of the leaves.

When using artichokes whole, rub them with a lemon to prevent discoloration.

When using slices of artichoke, cut it first in half, then in quarters or wedges.

Cut out the choke and discard it.

As the slices are cut, put them in cold water with the juice of a lemon. Drain well and pat dry before cooking.

until they snap as they break away. Cut off the bottoms of the stems and peel back with a paring knife, over the point where the leaf broke off, to get to the outside of the heart of the artichoke. Turn the artichoke around and cut about one-third off the top of the remaining leaves. Pare all the way around the top to cut off any remaining fibrous parts. Slice the artichoke lengthwise into quarters, exposing the thistlelike choke. Cut it out. Then slice the quarters lengthwise into halves or thirds. As one by one the artichokes are prepared, put them in water with the juice of 1 lemon to keep them from discoloring.

EGGPLANTS come in various shapes, sizes, and hues of purple. The most commonly available types are a small elongated one and a larger, more rounded one. For dishes that call for cubed eggplant, we use the smaller ones; for those that need lengthwise slices, we use the larger variety. Either way, a good eggplant must be firm, with a taut and shiny skin which is an integral part of the vegetable and should not be peeled off. If overripe or stored too long, they, especially the larger ones, develop tough skins and pulpy, seedy insides.

The preparation of the eggplant before cooking is simple but necessary. The vegetable must be cut either in half or into slices, salted, and left to drain, standing vertically in a colander or spread out on the counter. This is to let the salt draw out the bitter humor of the eggplant, which takes about 20 minutes for the smaller slices of eggplant, half an hour for the thicker halves. As they sit, the salt first becomes damp and then completely wet. When the time is up, scrape off the moisture with a knife, give a gentle squeeze to the eggplant, rinse briefly under running water, pat dry, and it is ready to proceed with further cutting, if necessary, and cooking.

TOMATOES for sauces should be the pear-shaped plum variety. They have to be totally ripe and red, soft to the touch and almost ready to disintegrate. In Italy they are prepared quite simply: washed clean and then cut into chunks — skin, seeds, pulp, juice,

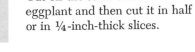

Cut off the stem end of the eggplant and then cut it in half or in ¼-inch-thick slices.

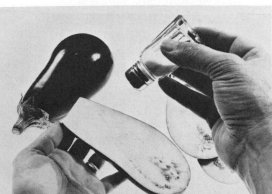

Salt the open surface of the slices and halves.

Put the salted slices or halves in a colander to drain for at least 20 to 30 minutes.

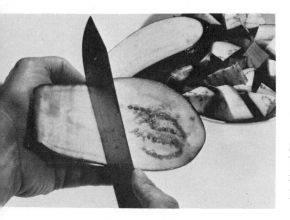

Scrape off the moist salt and bitter juice and the eggplant is ready to be cooked any way you wish.

and all — directly over the pan or pot they'll be cooked in. This saves time as well as juice. In some instances people who do not believe in roughage or in the age-old proverb, *"ciò che non am-mazza, ingrassa,"* — what doesn't kill you fattens you — peel their tomatoes. The method is as follows: the tomatoes are first blanched in boiling water for a minute or two, and then are skinned and seeded or passed through a food mill. The peasant style of peeling is even simpler: wash your hands and with your fingers squeeze the tomatoes through a fine mesh sieve. You get all the juice and pulp.

If fresh plum tomatoes aren't available, use the canned, whole, peeled plum or pear-shaped tomatoes. Be sure they are marked "tomatoes with added tomato juice, salt, calcium salt, and citric acid." (You do not want those packed in tomato puree.) These tomatoes are more than adequate and, above all, are available everywhere all year round. Some plum tomatoes are canned crushed but they are second-best, because they have been put up with a significant amount of tomato puree which gives them a sharper taste.

Stewed tomatoes in cans or salad tomatoes are not adequate for our sauces because they are too watery, sometimes sweet, and do not boil down to the right consistency. As for tomato paste, remember that it is a concentrate: use with discretion and dilute with warm water or broth. It gives sauces a deep red color but if overused produces a sharp, too tomatoey taste, the kind that can give Italian cooking a bad name.

Tomatoes for salads are another type altogether. We recommend, however, that when possible you use the home-grown salad species. Their size may be uneven but, oh, what character they have. For a really Italian treat, choose ones that are not totally ripe, but are rather a reddish pink with shades of green still on top. Once they are cut and on the table their fragrance and taste will enchant you. Their individuality can't even be compared with the intensively grown, perfectly shaped, same-size, same-untaste tomatoes grown commercially and ripened unnaturally in packages.

TRUFFLES are subterranean mushroomlike plants, piquant and aromatic, a gourmet experience since Greek and Roman times. They are, perhaps, an acquired taste, as some people consider them too strong in both flavor and aroma. But, like the proverbial mountain, they are there and waiting to be explored. They are found in very few places in the United States and must be hunted in the ground around the roots of trees with the aid of a truffle-hunting dog or pig. Most truffles come to the American consumer in cans imported for sale by specialty shops at necessarily high prices, but how you acquire them is beside the point here (just buy from a reputable store). Suppose you are now the proud owner of one or more white (from Piedmont) or black (from Umbria or Perigord, France) truffles. Keeping them in a safe won't do anything for you or the truffles. We respectfully suggest you use them with cheese or rice or pasta and offer one recommendation: use also the best ungrated and seasoned Parmesan or *grana* cheese (hard, dry, but not dried out), and the best olive oil. If you happen to be where fresh truffles are available, they are superior to canned. A dish made with fresh truffles could be one of the eating experiences of your life. Canned or fresh, truffle preparation is simple: slice them tissue-paper thin with a paring knife, or, should you happen to have one, a truffle slicer.

ZUCCHINI is another vegetable in which bigness doesn't necessarily mean goodness, but freshness does. A good zucchini has a smooth, taut skin and when held in the hand (no poking or squeezing, please) feels heavy and full. New, very small zucchini (less than 4 inches) are good marinated or in omelets. If they're right from the garden, they're good raw. The average size (5 to 7 inches) is good for just about everything. Anything longer than 8 inches should be stuffed or filled only. The insides of these bigger ones are pulpier and more full of seeds, and the skin is inclined to be a bit tough, but trimmed properly, stuffed well, baked with or without a sauce, they can hold their own with the smaller ones.

Preparing a zucchini is merely a matter of washing it, cutting off a bit of each end, and removing any bruises. Coring small or medium-sized zucchini is rather like coring an apple: use an apple corer or the longer zucchini corer. If using a huge zucchini, cut it into slices 2 inches thick and core each slice. The inner pulp cuts out easily with a paring knife. Stuffed slices, rather than one great whole or two big halves, simplify cooking and serving.

AROMI E SPEZIE / FLAVORINGS

HERBS, SPICES, AND FLAVORINGS in the typical Italian kitchen, contrary to widespread belief, are used discreetly. Part of the wisdom of good Italian cooks — or any other for that matter — is their economical and selective use of ingredients. They let each element do its best without having to fight another and they neither mix flavors and aromas indiscriminately into an undistinguishable entity, nor do they allow any single one to be so overpowering that it numbs the taste buds.

BASIL, PARSLEY, SAGE, the three most commonly used herbs, have without doubt a better flavor when fresh. A dried version is an approximation of the green. Basil and parsley lose a good deal of their fragrance when dried, while sage seems to acquire a sharpness that bears little resemblance to the mellow, smooth aroma and taste of the fresh herb; all three after a certain shelf life taste and smell like dried hay. So, if you must use the dried product, you must, but in doing so be especially careful in measuring and keep track of its age. While fresh parsley is generally available in most markets year round, the other two herbs are not, but there is a solution. Any suitable patch of soil in the sun or a window box or a flowerpot can yield a rewarding crop of herbs. Parsley plants are biennials and grow to about a foot in height. Flat-leaved or Italian parsley is more flavorful than the ordinary curly kind, seems sturdier, and withstands the cold better. Both can winter indoors the first season of their lives. Basil, on the other hand, is an annual, and to keep it all year long one has to start afresh every three or four months. Fresh basil leaves from an abundant summer crop (from plants that grow anywhere from one to three feet) can be kept in olive oil in sealed pint jars for months and used as you wish. When it comes to measuring fresh herbs such as parsley and basil, our quantities refer to what we think is average size. Roughly speaking, 2 of our sprigs of parsley produce 1 tablespoon of finely chopped parsley (5 sprigs = 1 cup loosely packed leaves = 3 tablespoons finely chopped). The size of our average basil leaf is just about the size of a soupspoon.

As for sage, it's a perennial plant, so pretty and hardy it should be in any flower garden. Its leaves can be picked from under a covering of snow and when used fresh make all the difference in the world.

If a recipe will be ruined by the use of a dried herb, such as dried basil for *pesto,* we will say so.

ROSEMARY is an herb that looks like twigs from a pine tree, and its perfume is vaguely resinous and reminiscent of the odor of pine. In temperate climates it keeps well year after year, a small shrub to decorate a garden. Fresh rosemary needles give off more aroma than dried and, clinging as they do to their twigs, are easier to remove from a dish before serving. Dried rosemary needles are stripped from their twigs and are therefore hard to remove from anything unless wrapped in cheesecloth during cooking. We hardly ever bother doing this anyway, because dried or fresh rosemary is equally welcome.

GARLIC, discretion should be thy name. Garlic should whisper, not shout its presence. With few exceptions, one or two cloves of garlic are used to flavor a dish. Even then, more times than not, the garlic clove is used whole or cut in half if large and sautéed briefly in olive oil until golden. The clove is then discarded after its flavoring job is done. In the event you crave a stronger garlic taste, you can sauté the cloves until more brown than golden (but not dark brown or they will leave a bitter, unpleasant taste). When a dish calls for finely chopped garlic, stick to the rule and really mince it. In the event a whole clove is left in a soup during its long simmer, skewer the garlic with a wooden toothpick. It's easier to find and remove at the end.

MARJORAM AND OREGANO, close cousins, are almost interchangeable in their fresh state, and when dried are frequently confused with each other. In theory, oregano is made from the dried tops of the wild plant and marjoram from the leaves of the domestic. Quite frankly, you can be sold one for the other with no malice intended, no harm suffered. Fresh marjoram leaves give the mildest, sweetest flavor; dried, powdered marjoram is a deeper version of the first; and though dried oregano is the sharpest of all, it is delightful and matchless if used sparingly.

CAPERS, the buds of a Mediterranean plant belonging to the mustard family, make frequent appearances in Italian dishes. They are available pickled or preserved in salt. Salted capers are to be preferred: the particular caper flavor and aroma has not been changed by the pickling vinegar, and they are usually cheaper. When using the salted, rinse them thoroughly in cold water and dry on a paper towel. If using pickled capers, be sure to drain them well. Capers sometimes can be used as a substitute for anchovies. Obviously they don't have exactly the same flavor but they perform the same duty: give saltiness and an extra fillip to a sauce or filling. So, if you have a thing about anchovies, 1 teaspoon of capers chopped into a paste is considered an equivalent to 1 minced anchovy fillet.

RED PEPPER, cousin to the black and white, is commonly called *peperoncino*, little pepper, or in some regions *diavoletto*, little devil. That's what it is. In Italy red pepper is sold dried and whole. In the United States it is frequently sold crushed, seeds included. Whole red pepper can be found in spice stores as well as in Italian and Chinese groceries and is to be preferred because a cook can control it more easily. The whole pod can be broken open, the seeds discarded, and pieces or all of the pod used to flavor a sauce or, more generally, the oil for a sauce. When flavoring oil, the rule of thumb is to let the pepper pod stay in the oil over medium heat until its color goes from bright orange-red to deep brown and then remove the pod. The longer red pepper stays in the oil, the hotter the flavor will be. If left in the oil too long, red pepper will make your sauce a fiery, lip-swelling affair. If you've never worked with red pepper in this manner, a bit of bread dipped in the flavored oil and tasted will help you to judge how much pepper flavor has been released.

Crushed red pepper, if used to flavor oil, can burn very easily and of course is difficult to remove. Burnt red pepper pod, or even worse its seeds, gives a bitter taste. If you must work with crushed red pepper, use it in moderation and add it half way along in the cooking of the sauce.

NUTMEG AND PEPPER, both Asian spices, deserve a special place in the Italian kitchen if for no other reason than that their popularity in ancient times led to the search for a new trade route to the Indies and thus, indirectly, to the discovery of America. We show our respect for them by using them freshly grated or ground. A fresh nutmeg is roughly the shape and size of a pecan, and can be grated on the fine side of an ordinary kitchen grater, or you can buy a special little nutmeg grater in the kitchenware shop. Either way you grate it, you'll find its perfume and taste far more distinctive than the powdered and packaged kind. Whole nutmegs are sold 7 or 8 to the jar, and while difficult to find in supermarkets are frequently marketed by companies that carry a specialty line of spices.

As for pepper, it comes in white as well as black peppercorns. The black are the whole berries of the plant; the white are the husked berries, and hence are milder in aroma but not in flavor. We suggest you keep two grinders on hand, one for black and one for white, adjusting to coarse grind for dishes where pepper really stars and to a fine grind for ordinary use. We prefer our white pepper finely ground in the dishes it enhances.

ANCHOVIES, aside from being a favorite and simple *antipasto,* are a popular seasoning in many Italian dishes. They are preserved whole, packed in salt, or are salted, filleted, and canned in olive oil. For use as a seasoning the salted ones are preferable because they disintegrate more thoroughly in the sauce they are to flavor. They can be found in Italian grocery stores and are sold either piecemeal from big tins and barrels or packed in small cans.

The cleaning of a salted anchovy is very simple: hold the fish (it is already headless) under a stream of cold, running water, brush off the excess salt and the skin with your fingers, open up the fish, pull off the tail and with it the backbone, and you have two fillets ready to work with.

If you can't get salted anchovies, buy the small cans of flat fillets (a 2-ounce can usually contains 12). They are as good in flavor but a little more firm in texture. Simply lift them out of the oil they're packed in and drain them.

TUNA, available in the Italian market, is packed in olive oil and is usually sold by weight from big cans. When it is to be used by itself, the average cook buys the more solid pieces taken from the darkest meat of the fish, the belly. When to be used for stuffing and sauces or broken up for salad, the less dark, less solid, and less expensive portions of the fish are chosen. We've found that if we can't get Italian tuna packed in small cans, American tuna, marked Chunk Light, and packed in vegetable oil, is a fair substitute in flavor and texture.

BURRO, OLIO, E FORMAGGIO /
BUTTER, OIL, AND CHEESE

BUTTER in Italy is made without salt. We prefer it this way and continue cooking with unsalted butter. It is more delicate and in the long run has the added advantage of allowing the cook to control the saltiness of a dish. All the recipes in this book that call for butter require unsalted butter. If you use lightly salted butter, adjust the amount of salt in your dish accordingly.

OLIVE OIL: when you speak of oil in Italy it's taken for granted you mean olive oil. Only the other oils, considered lesser, get specifications. Olive oil does have several denominations, depending on the various pressings of the olives. The first pressing is the best; it makes Pure Virgin Olive Oil and by law should be so labeled. Subsequent pressings are labeled Pure Olive Oil, and then simply Olive Oil. After that, labeling becomes a game of word-acrobatics when describing mixtures of different pressings or even combinations of olive oil with percentages of vegetable oils. Such percentages should be checked in the fine print of the labels. It makes an interesting and amusing exercise. We have found "100% imported olive oil" where the 100 percent referred to the word "imported" and the fine print specified it was 10 percent olive oil and 90 percent vegetable oil. Good olive oil, incidentally, is not all imported: California also produces a quality product, but it seems to be preserved jealously for local markets. Real, good, pure olive oil is expensive, yet a little goes a long way: it is more viscous than vegetable oil and has more flavor. Good olive oil should be transparent gold with a hint of pale green in its color. It has a delicate but definite taste, and lingers briefly on the palate. An olive taste that's too strong doesn't make a good olive oil at all. Perhaps the best advice is to buy a small quantity, dip a bit of Italian bread in it, and taste. If it delights the palate, it's perfect. If it leaves a bitter aftertaste, it is also perfect — to boil in cauldrons and pour on attacking enemies. You get a castle for that.

CHEESE: it is unfortunate that only a few of the many delicious Italian cheeses are known in this country. For cooking purposes, however, the ones most commonly used are usually available, produced domestically or imported: *parmigiano* or Parmesan, *pecorino* or Romano, *mozzarella*, and *ricotta*.

PARMESAN AND ROMANO: Parmesan is made of cow's milk, and the best of its kind was and is made in Parma, hence the name; *pecorino*, sheep's milk cheese (*pecora* is the word for sheep in Italian), is commonly known here as Romano, because of the especially good *pecorino* produced in the Roman countryside.

Both cheeses are at their best when perfectly aged but not dried out. Ungrated, they are used as table cheese, the Parmesan being a distinctly flavored mellow cheese, the Romano much sharper. When used in cooking they should be grated just as needed and not a moment before.

However, in this vast country of ours it is not always possible to find good ungrated Parmesan or Romano, and generally the good ones are imported and so expensive that they must be regarded as luxuries, something to treat yourself to occasionally. On the other hand, the grated domestic ones are readily available and (we are whispering to save the sanity of the purist) we think acceptable to the cooking and the purse — with a word of advice. Make sure that the grated cheese has not been sitting on a shelf too long (the container should have an expiration date) and has therefore become totally dry: grated cheese loses its aroma fast, so once you open a container, transfer its contents to a glass jar with a good sealing top and keep refrigerated. Sometimes a mixture of Parmesan and Romano is available, but we do not advise your buying it. If you like a mixture of the flavors (and this is not frequently called for), keep the two cheeses separate until the moment of use, and then mix to your own taste.

MOZZARELLA is a fresh, soft cheese, rarely available in its authentic form in the United States, though it does appear sometimes in specialty markets and Italian food stores. Real *mozzarella* can be cut with a fork and is a very delicate cheese to be eaten fresh or cooked in a variety of dishes. When cooked it becomes creamy and it remains so as it cools off. The *mozzarella* most commonly found here is made with whole milk or part skim milk; it is a semi-hard cheese that melts quite nicely but in cooling solidifies into a rubbery state. The simplest way to avoid this is to use it not in slices but shredded on the coarse side of a cheese grater. When possible, use whole milk *mozzarella* for a softer texture, richer flavor.

RICOTTA is a spoonable, very mild cheese used in Italian cooking from North to South, in everything from *antipasti* to *dolci*. It is more and more available in markets throughout this country. Quite perishable, it should be kept not much more than three days in the refrigerator. Like Parmesan cheese, its container should carry an expiration date. Cottage cheese should not be substituted for *ricotta* because the two are miles apart in both taste and texture. Cottage cheese is salty and holds its curdlike texture, while *ricotta* is not salty and is smooth, almost like heavy whipped cream. In southern Italy, however, *ricotta* is also salted and dried into a semihard cheese similar to Greek feta cheese. This variation is called *Ricotta salata* or *Primo sale* or *Caciotta salata*.

SUGHI E SALSE / BASIC SAUCES

The trouble with languages such as English and Italian is that words like *sughi* and *salse* translate into one word: sauces. There's really a thin line of distinction between the two. In general, a *sugo* is an integral part of a dish, e.g., *pasta al sugo di pomodoro* is pasta AND tomato sauce. *Salsa* is an enrichment or accompaniment of a dish, e.g., *pomodori con la maionese,* tomatoes WITH mayonnaise sauce.

Of the very long list of sauces in the Italian kitchen, there are a few which can be considered basic and which appear in a variety of preparations, so we group recipes for them here, preceded by a bit of general advice:

To simmer a sauce, even briefly, the heat must be low and even. If a sauce cooks too hard and fast, its liquid evaporates before its flavors have blended properly and it becomes too thick too soon. If this happens, a bit of hot (not cold) water (or broth, if called for) should be added, enabling the simmering to continue the correct length of time to get the right flavor and consistency.

To reach sauce consistency, simmer until the sauce is reduced in liquid and just thick enough to coat the spoon that stirs it. It should be a bit darker in color than when the cooking started and well amalgamated — all the ingredients nicely blended in texture and taste. In cooking meatless sauces this state is reached in a relatively short time. If using a sauce to poach large fish steaks or eggs, the sauce should be half cooked before adding the main ingredient of the dish.

To check a sauce's seasonings, take advantage of a morsel of Italian bread. Dip it into the simmering sauce, taste, and then decide about salt and pepper. After all, a sauce is always eaten ON something, and tasting it unaccompanied makes no sense. Some ingredients, such as capers and anchovies, vary in saltiness, so a check is especially necessary.

BESCIAMELLA / WHITE SAUCE

This is the white sauce used in *lasagne, cannelloni,* and casseroles. This recipe makes enough for a large *lasagne* and is of medium consistency.

    8 tablespoons unsalted butter
    ¾ cup quick-mixing flour
    4 cups milk
    1 teaspoon freshly grated nutmeg
    ¾ teaspoon salt
    freshly ground white pepper

Melt the butter in a heavy saucepan over low heat. Add the flour all at once, and stir rapidly with a wire whisk until blended.

Heat the milk to scalding, and add it all at once to the butter-flour mixture, stirring vigorously with the wire whisk. Continue cooking over medium heat, stirring constantly, until the sauce has thickened and is smooth, about the consistency of a thin pudding. Add the nutmeg, salt, and pepper.

Cool the *besciamella* for about 15 minutes before using. It becomes firmer as it cools.

MAIONESE / MAYONNAISE

True Italian *maionese,* according to experts, should be made by hand, but, in the interest of the cook who is short on time, here is how it can be done in a blender. A more tangy mayonnaise is hard to find. This makes enough for 6 normal *maionese* eaters. It easily doubles for those who can't resist.

    1 egg (at room temperature)
    juice of ½ lemon
    ¼ teaspoon salt

finely ground white pepper, to taste

¾ cup olive oil

Break the whole egg into the blender. Add the lemon juice, salt, white pepper, and 3 tablespoons of the olive oil. Blend until the mixture is thick, light colored, and uniform. Keep the blender going and pour the rest of the olive oil in a slow, steady trickle into the vortex of the mixture. Stop pouring only if a small bubble of oil forms in the center, at which point you blend without adding any more oil until the bubble disappears. Then resume pouring in the remaining oil, in a steady trickle as before. Blend a moment more, and use as you will. For 6.

PESTO / BASIL-NUT-GARLIC SAUCE

Pesto means pounded, and in this case a combination of nuts, basil leaves, and cheeses are crushed together until, when mixed with olive oil, the paste becomes a sauce, Genoa's grand contribution to pasta and soups. It has an incredible flavor, hard to describe.

Any good Genovese would have a fainting spell at the thought of substituting a modern blender for the traditional mortar and pestle used to make *pesto*, but if you're strapped for time, here is the old as well as the new or blender version.

Pesto may be made with more or less garlic, depending on taste, but the proportions below produce a flavor in which the basil, garlic, and pine nuts share equally.

2 cups loosely packed fresh (NOT dried) basil leaves

2 medium garlic cloves

1 teaspoon salt

3 ounces pine nuts

1 tablespoon grated Parmesan cheese

1 tablespoon grated Romano cheese

¾ to 1 cup olive oil

If using a mortar: mix together the basil, garlic, and salt, and chop them to fine bits. Crush the pine nuts with a rolling pin or meat pounder, and add them to the garlic and basil. Chop some more and then put everything into a large mortar. Pound and grind the mixture until a good thick paste is formed. Add the cheeses, and grind some more until they are well blended in. Add the olive oil 1 tablespoon at a time, working with the pestle until the paste has absorbed as much oil as it can. Depending on how moist the cheeses and the basil leaves are, you may need to use a little more or a little less oil to reach a thick sauce consistency.

If using a blender: coarsely chop the basil leaves and put them in the blender with the salt. Blend at low speed for a few seconds, then add the other ingredients but only half the olive oil.

Blend at medium speed until everything is minutely minced but not pureed (an important part of *pesto* is its texture). During blending stop the machine every once in a while and scrape the mixture down from the sides and out of the bottom corners.

Pour the mixture into a suitable container and add the remaining oil. Blend by hand until the oil is perfectly amalgamated.

Pesto keeps for a long time if placed in a jar. Before you seal it make sure a thin layer of oil has formed on the top of the *pesto,* and if it hasn't add a few drops of oil yourself. For 6.

SALSA DI POMODORO / BASIC TOMATO SAUCE

4 tablespoons olive oil
4 cups peeled plum tomatoes
1 carrot
1 celery stalk
1 onion
3 or 4 fresh parsley sprigs
3 or 4 fresh basil leaves
2 teaspoons salt, or to taste
freshly ground pepper to taste

Put the olive oil into a big saucepan, and cut the plum tomatoes into bite-sized chunks over the pan (so that no juice is wasted). Coarsely chop the other vegetables and herbs, and add everything to the olive oil. Bring to a boil, lower the heat, cover, and simmer for about ½ hour. Uncover, taste for salt, adjust the seasonings if necessary, and simmer another 15 minutes or so, or until the liquid has reduced and the tomatoes have practically disintegrated. Put the whole mixture through a sieve or food mill, and use it as you wish. If the sauce seems runny after being sieved, return it to the heat and simmer it until further condensed. For 6.

SALSA VERDE / GREEN SAUCE

This sauce of parsley, garlic, and capers, bound together with oil and lemon, embellishes any fish in the market. It can be made in a blender if you are absolutely sure you can trust yourself to stop blending before all the little bits of herbs are ground to a puree. *Salsa verde* minced by hand obviously takes more time to make and has an interestingly varied texture, compared to the blended version, which is creamy. Frankly, we recommend the handmade sauce.

Salsa verde can be made ahead of time and keeps well in the refrigerator with an extra drop or two of olive oil on top. It must, however, be brought to room temperature and stirred before serving.

    2 cups parsley leaves
    2 tablespoons capers (preferably salted, not pickled)
    1 garlic clove (optional for fish)
    ⅛ teaspoon salt, or to taste
    ½ cup olive oil
    juice of 1½ lemons

If making by hand: chop the parsley, capers, and garlic coarsely, add the salt, and mince together thoroughly. Put the resulting mixture in a mortar and grind to a paste. In the absence of a mortar, mince everything as finely as possible, put into a bowl, and stir in the oil. Add the olive oil, 1 tablespoon at a time, and keep on grinding until a very thick sauce consistency is reached. Then add the lemon juice a little at a time in order to dilute the sauce until it is really spoonable. Taste for salt and adjust the seasonings if necessary.

If making in the blender: chop the parsley, capers, and garlic coarsely, and put them in a blender with the lemon juice and the salt. Add half the olive oil and blend at low speed for 10 seconds or until the parsley looks minced. Add the rest of the oil and blend for 3 seconds. Pour into a suitable bowl, stir, and taste for salt. If the capers haven't added enough salt, adjust the seasonings. For 6.

SALSA VERDE PIEMONTESE /
GREEN SAUCE, PIEDMONTESE STYLE

1 salted anchovy, or 2 canned fillets
3 cups loosely packed parsley leaves
2 garlic cloves
2 thick slices (2 ounces) day-old Italian bread
⅓ cup wine vinegar
2 to 6 tablespoons olive oil
freshly ground pepper
salt to taste

If using the salted anchovy, fillet it (page 15); if using canned fillets, drain them.

Chop together thoroughly the parsley, garlic, and anchovies.

After trimming the crusts off the bread, soak it 3 or 4 minutes in the vinegar. Squeeze out the vinegar, and shred the bread into a small mixing bowl. Add the chopped parsley mixture, and mix with a wooden spoon, mashing everything against the side of the bowl until well amalgamated. Add 1 tablespoon of the olive oil and mix again.

If using *salsa verde* for stuffing tomatoes (page 38) add 1 more tablespoon of oil and mix well.

If using this sauce for poached fish, add 4 more tablespoons of olive oil, or a total of 6, which is enough to make a pourable sauce.

Taste for salt and add some if necessary. Add freshly ground pepper. For 6.

ANTIPASTI

APPETIZERS

THE ANTIPASTO, both in name (*ante prandium* — before the meal) and tradition, comes straight from the ancient Romans. Since it is actually nothing more than a gastronomic exercise in preparation for the *prandium,* the meal, it has to be a tasty morsel. It should tease the appetite, not exhaust it. When the Romans had a feast, a real banquet, the modest *antipasto* became a course in itself called the *frigida mensa,* the cold table, a succession of cold dishes before the hot ones. What remains of this tradition is today's custom of serving most *antipasti* cold. As a rule, the *antipasto* is not part of an everyday family menu and is reserved for special occasions. Theoretically it should not appear on meatless days or days of fasting and penance, but if an occasion arises, go ahead and have a fling.

Here are a few *antipasti* we particularly like for their taste and simplicity. Our selection can be augmented by some dishes we list elsewhere as second courses or *contorni:*

Peperoni alla Clara (pages 180–181)
Pomodori ripieni al forno (pages 181–182)
Zucchine all marchigiana (pages 190–191)
Zucchine ripiene al tonno (page 191)
Cipolle ripiene (pages 214–215)

When certain *antipasti* can double as second courses, we've said so in the individual recipes.

BAGNA CAUDA /
HOT SAUCE WITH RAW VEGETABLES

This sauce is hot in temperature, not in taste.

The actual quantities and types of vegetables to be dipped in it are the cook's choice and must depend on what is in season, but the amount and variety given below will serve 6. Cardoons are rarely found in our local market, but seeds for the home garden are sold in various parts of the country. They are a perennial Mediterranean plant similar to celery and their stalks are used as a vegetable throughout Italy. If you can't find them, just skip them. The peppers should be meaty, the celery stalks white and from the center of the bunch, and the cauliflower should be small and tender.

VEGETABLES
5 cardoons, with 1 lemon
1 red sweet pepper
1 green sweet pepper
5 celery stalks
½ head cauliflower
5 small carrots
5 or 6 cabbage leaves

SAUCE
6 garlic cloves
½ cup milk
5 tablespoons unsalted butter
12 anchovy fillets
1 cup olive oil
salt to taste

Ahead of time: wash the cardoons, peel off the stringiest ribs, cut them into 3-inch pieces and soak in water for an hour with the juice of the lemon; peel the garlic cloves and soak them in the milk for an hour, to cut their sharpness.

Melt the butter over very low heat in an earthenware casserole. Mince the garlic, or press it, and sauté it in the butter for 5 minutes. Mash the anchovies into a paste and stir it into the butter. Slowly stir in the olive oil. Continue cooking over very low heat, stirring occasionally for 35 to 40 minutes. Add salt to taste.

While the sauce is cooking, prepare the rest of the vegetables. Core the peppers and cut them into thin strips. Wash the celery stalks and cut them in half lengthwise. Break the cauliflower into flowerets. Peel the carrots and cut them into lengthwise strips. Cut the cabbage open and use about half of its most tender leaves, cutting them into manageable strips.

When the sauce is ready, transfer it from the stove to a warming device on the table. It must be kept warm while everyone dips his vegetable pieces in it. And here is where *Bagna cauda* (hot bath) gets its name. Dipping can be done either with the fingers or, perhaps an unnecessary refinement, with long forks like those used for fondue. *Bagna cauda* should be accompanied by a full-bodied, dry red wine such as Barbera, Barolo, or a Burgundy. For 6.

BISTECCHE DEI POVERI / POOR MAN'S STEAKS

These steaks are in reality slices of eggplant, which are grilled and brushed with herb-flavored olive oil as they cook and after they are done. In Sicily *bistecche* like these are served as an *antipasto*, a *contorno*, or, when a charcoal fire is going, as one of many dishes in a mixed grill.

3 medium eggplants (about 2 pounds)
salt
½ cup olive oil

2 teaspoons oregano
2 tablespoons coarsely chopped fresh mint (about 40 leaves)

Start your outdoor grill.

Cut the eggplants into lengthwise slices about ¼ inch thick. (Throw away the outermost, curved slice, which is mostly skin.) Prepare as usual (pages 7–9).

While the eggplants are standing, mix the olive oil with the oregano and chopped mint leaves.

When the fire is ready, take as many slices as will fit on your grill, brush them on one side only with the flavored oil, and put them on to brown oiled-side down. While they are grilling, brush their top sides with more oil. When a slice is brown on one side, turn and brown the other side. When done on both sides, remove to a serving platter, brushing with just a bit more oil, and keep warm until all the slices are cooked. Serve hot. For 6.

BURRO E ALICI / SWEET BUTTER AND ANCHOVIES

In Rome, when someone asks "How's it going?" the answer is "*a burro e alici*," which means it couldn't be better, as smooth as sweet butter yet with enough flavor to be interesting. That is what this simple *antipasto* is all about.

6 salted anchovies, or 12 canned fillets
6 slices fresh Italian bread
6 tablespoons unsalted butter

If using salted anchovies, fillet them (page 15); if using canned, drain them.

Spread the bread slices generously with the butter and top with the fillets, 2 to a slice. Serve with a glass of chilled, dry white wine. And double the quantities if you wish. For 6.

3 medium eggplants (about 2 pounds)
salt
½ cup olive oil
2 onions
1½ pounds peeled plum tomatoes, fresh or canned
2 celery stalks
1 tablespoon capers
12 large green cracked olives
½ cup wine vinegar
1 tablespoon sugar

Cut the eggplants into halves and prepare as usual (pages 7–9). After desalting them, cut them into 1-inch cubes. Sauté in 5 tablespoons of the olive oil in a large frying pan over medium heat for about 10 minutes, or until golden and slightly limp.

The sauce is prepared separately. Peel the onions and cut them into thin slivers. Sauté until limp in the remaining olive oil in another big frying pan over medium heat. Cut the tomatoes into chunks, and add to the onions. Simmer for 5 minutes.

Chop the celery into ½-inch dice. Add the celery, capers, and olives to the simmering tomato sauce. Bring to a boil, add the eggplant, and return the sauce to a boil. Add the vinegar and sugar and cook another 5 minutes, or until the vinegar has evaporated. Do not overcook; one of the pleasures of this dish is its texture. Serve hot or cold. For 6.

FUNGHI ALL'INSALATA /
MARINATED MUSHROOMS

1 pound mushrooms
1 garlic clove
½ cup olive oil
juice of 2 lemons

2 tablespoons chopped fresh parsley
freshly ground pepper
salt to taste

Clean (and peel if necessary) the mushrooms and cut them into very thin slices.

Rub a shallow serving bowl or deep platter with the garlic clove. Spread the raw mushroom slices evenly in the bowl. Add the olive oil and the lemon juice, and sprinkle with the parsley. Add salt, about 1 teaspoon or to taste, and twist the pepper mill 4 or 5 times over all. Tip the platter and thoroughly baste the mushrooms with the dressing so that the slices are really coated. Refrigerate for at least ½ hour before serving. For 6.

INSALATA DI FUNGHI TORINESE /
MUSHROOM SALAD

1 pound fresh mushrooms
1 garlic clove
¼ cup chopped fresh parsley
3 salted anchovies, or 6 canned fillets
2 large egg yolks
½ to ¾ cup olive oil
juice of 1½ lemons
salt to taste

If the mushrooms aren't spotless, wash them carefully and dry on paper towels. Cut into thin wedges and put them in a serving bowl large enough to toss them in.

Cut the garlic clove in two and wipe a small mixing bowl with the halves, pressing out as much juice as possible.

If using salted anchovies, fillet them (page 15); if using canned, drain them. Finely chop the parsley and anchovy fillets together and put them in the mixing bowl. Beat the egg yolks well and add them to the parsley. Add the olive oil and the lemon juice. Stir with a fork (always stirring in the same direction) until the mixture is thickened and creamy. Salt to taste.

Pour the sauce over the mushrooms, toss gently, and serve. This can be used as a *contorno* as well as an *antipasto*. For 6.

PEPERONI AL TONNO /
BAKED PEPPERS STUFFED WITH TUNA

3 to 4 thick slices of day-old Italian bread
1 7-ounce can Italian tuna
2 dozen (pitted) Sicilian black olives (packed in brine, not dried)
6 sweet peppers (red, green, or yellow)
4 tablespoons olive oil, minimum
¼ teaspoon salt
¼ teaspoon freshly ground pepper

Preheat the oven to 400°.

Soak the stale bread briefly under running water. Squeeze it well, discard the crusts, and shred the remaining bread into a bowl.

Drain the tuna, and chop together coarsely with the olives. Add to the shredded bread. Moisten the mixture with enough olive oil to make it cling together. Add the salt and pepper and mix well.

Wash the peppers, cut them in half lengthwise, and remove seeds and cores. Fill the halves with the tuna mixture and put them in an oiled baking dish.

Bake (at 400°) 15 to 20 minutes, or until the peppers are tender to a fork. Serve cold as an *antipasto* or hot as a second course. For 6.

PEPERONI ARROSTO / ROAST PEPPERS

This is an old, familiar favorite, so popular in Italy that no cookbook of Italian food would be complete without it.

    6 to 8 large sweet peppers (green, yellow, or red)
    juice of 2 lemons
    8 tablespoons olive oil
    salt to taste

If using a gas stove: turn the grates of the burners upside down to cradle the peppers and set the flame at medium high. Put the peppers on the grates. As soon as a side is blackened, turn the pepper and roast another part. Keep turning them all until the outer skins are blackened and blistered.

If using an electric stove: put the peppers in the broiler, as close to the heating coil as possible, and keep turning them as they blacken. Roast until the outer skins are completely charred.

Put the peppers under a cold stream of water and peel off the black with your fingers.

Cut off the top stems, take out the seeds, and slice the peppers lengthwise into ¼- to ½-inch-wide strips. Drain briefly and put in a serving dish. Pour the lemon juice over the peppers. Add the olive oil and salt to taste. Baste well.

The peppers can be served right away, but they improve if they marinate for ½ hour or so. For 6.

PEPERONI RIPIENI ALLA PIEMONTESE /
BAKED PEPPERS STUFFED WITH RICE

    6 large sweet peppers (green, yellow, or red)
    1½ cups long-grain rice
    1½ teaspoons salt
    ½ cup chopped fresh parsley
    3 garlic cloves

½ cup olive oil
3 canned anchovy fillets, or 1 tablespoon capers and 3 olives
1 tablespoon unsalted butter

Preheat the oven to 325°.

Cut the peppers in half lengthwise. After removing seeds and cores, put the shells in boiling, salted water to cook for 5 minutes. Remove from the water and drain.

Put the rice in 3 cups of water with the salt. Bring to a boil, stir, cover, and cook for 10 minutes. Drain off any water that may remain.

Chop the parsley and garlic together until nearly a paste. Add it with 5 tablespoons of the olive oil to the still hot rice and stir well.

Mash the anchovies into the butter and cook the mixture with the remaining olive oil in a small frying pan over low heat until the butter has melted and the anchovies have disintegrated. (If using capers and olives, chop them to a paste and add to the oil and butter. Cook only until butter is melted.)

Fill the pepper halves with the rice mixture and put them in an oven-proof casserole or baking pan just large enough to hold them snugly. Spoon a bit of the flavored oil-butter mixture onto each pepper. Put ¼ cup water in the bottom of the pan to prevent the peppers from sticking and bake (at 325°) for ½ hour. Serve cold as an *antipasto* or hot as a side dish. For 6.

POMODORI AL TONNO /
TOMATOES STUFFED WITH TUNA

6 medium-sized, firm salad tomatoes
2 hardboiled eggs
1 3½-ounce can Italian tuna
1 tablespoon capers
1 tablespoon chopped fresh parsley
freshly ground white pepper
1 recipe *Maionese* (pages 20–21)

Cut the tops off the tomatoes. Scoop out the seeds and pulp and strain through a sieve, reserving the juice. Salt the tomato shells lightly and turn them upside down to drain.

Chop the edible part of the tomato tops. Finely chop the hard-boiled eggs and put in a mixing bowl with the tuna, capers, and parsley. Mix well. Add the chopped tomato tops and enough of the reserved tomato juice to make a paste.

Add half the mayonnaise to the tuna-egg paste, mix well, and stuff the tomato shells. Top with the remaining mayonnaise. Chill for ½ hour before serving. If the stuffed tomatoes are to be chilled longer, cover them with aluminum foil.

This makes a good second course as well as an *antipasto*. For 6.

POMODORI RIPIENI CON SALSA VERDE PIEMONTESE / STUFFED TOMATOES WITH GREEN SAUCE

6 medium-sized, firm salad tomatoes
2 hardboiled eggs
1 recipe *Salsa verde piemontese* (pages 24–25), made with 2
    tablespoons of olive oil
1 tablespoon olive oil

Cut the tomatoes into halves, scoop out the seeds, and turn the halves upside down to drain.

Peel the hardboiled eggs and remove the yolks. Chop the egg whites very finely.

To the *salsa verde piemontese* add the hardboiled egg yolks, mash, and mix well. Add the chopped egg whites, and mix again. Add 1 more tablespoon of olive oil, and mix until the sauce is thick and smooth.

Fill the drained tomato halves with the sauce-egg mixture, and chill for ½ hour. For 6.

POMODORI RIPIENI ALL'UMBRA /
STUFFED TOMATOES, UMBRIAN STYLE

6 firm but ripe salad tomatoes
1 teaspoon salt, or to taste
1 cup unseasoned coarse bread crumbs
¼ teaspoon freshly ground pepper
1 cup coarsely chopped fresh parsley
1 garlic clove
4 tablespoons olive oil
2 large eggs

Preheat the oven to 400°.

Cut the tomatoes into halves. Remove the seeds and pulp, and press through a strainer into a small bowl. Save the resulting juice. Salt the tomato halves lightly and turn them upside down on a plate or cutting board to drain.

Put the bread crumbs in a bowl and add the pepper and the remaining salt. Chop together the parsley and the garlic and add to the bread crumbs. Add the olive oil and the eggs and mix well. If the mixture is very stiff, add a tablespoon or so of the reserved tomato juice.

Fill the tomato shells with the mixture, and put them in an oiled baking dish. Bake (at 400°) for 30 minutes, spooning a bit more tomato juice on the stuffing during the baking. Serve either hot or cold as a second course as well as an *antipasto*. For 6.

POMODORI RIPIENI AI FUNGHI /
TOMATOES STUFFED WITH MUSHROOMS

6 to 8 large, firm salad tomatoes
1 small onion
5 parsley sprigs
1 celery stalk

4 tablespoons butter
½ pound mushrooms
1½ teaspoons salt
freshly ground pepper
3 slices day-old Italian bread
6 tablespoons grated Parmesan cheese
1 egg
5 tablespoons unseasoned bread crumbs

Preheat the oven to 350°.

Cut the tops off the tomatoes, scoop out the seeds, and pass both tops and insides through a sieve or food mill, saving the juice. Salt the tomato shells lightly and turn them upside down to drain while preparing the filling.

FILLING: chop together very finely the onion, parsley, and celery, and sauté in the butter in a frying pan over medium heat for 5 minutes, or until limp. Slice the mushrooms and add them to the pan. Add the salt and pepper and continue cooking.

Remove the crusts from the bread, soak the slices briefly in the reserved tomato juice, squeeze out the juice, and shred the bread into the pan. When the mushrooms have become limp, add ¾ cup of the tomato juice, and stir and cook another 3 minutes, or until the bread has disintegrated.

Remove the mushroom mixture from the heat and, when it has cooled slightly, stir in 4 tablespoons of the Parmesan cheese, one tablespoon at a time. Beat the egg slightly and combine it thoroughly with the mushroom mixture, and then fill the tomato shells. Mix the remaining Parmesan with the bread crumbs and sprinkle it on top of the stuffing.

Put the tomatoes in a casserole just large enough to accommodate them. Pour the remaining tomato juice into the bottom of the casserole to the depth of ½ inch. Bake ½ hour (at 350°). Serve hot. This also makes a nice second course. For 6.

ZUCCHINE MARINATE / MARINATED ZUCCHINI

6 medium zucchini
⅔ cup olive oil
¼ cup coarsely chopped fresh parsley
1 garlic clove
½ teaspoon salt
freshly ground pepper to taste
1 cup wine vinegar
1 red pepper pod, seeded (optional)

Wash the zucchini thoroughly, cut off the ends, and peel off any bruises or blemishes. Slice into ⅛-inch rounds.

Heat the olive oil in a medium-sized frying pan, and fry the zucchini slices in batches so that no more than one layer fries at a time. When they are golden brown, transfer zucchini slices to a shallow serving dish.

Chop together finely the parsley and garlic, and sprinkle over the fried zucchini. Sprinkle on the salt and pepper.

Heat the vinegar to a boil and pour it over the zucchini. (If you wish to add a "hot" touch to the dish, sink the seedless pepper pod in the middle, but remember to remove it before serving.) Tilt the dish back and forth a couple of times to make sure the garlic and parsley are well distributed. Marinate for at least 3 hours or, still better, all day. Serve cold as an *antipasto*, or as a side dish with poached or grilled fish. For 6.

PRIMI PIATTI

FIRST COURSES

THE PRIMO PIATTO carries the delightful burden of setting the pace for the rest of the meal. As a matter of fact, the *primo piatto* is the lion's share of a meatless meal. In other cuisines this course generally is a soup but the Italian *cucina* enlarges it into several families of dishes. Your choice of family was traditionally suggested by the season and region, but modern marketing techniques make most products available in all regions and often in all seasons. The choice has now become mostly a matter of personal preference. Here then are the six families:

1) *pasta asciutta:* those types of pasta (either commercially produced and packaged, or homemade) which have been cooked in boiling salted water, drained (thus becoming *asciutta,* or dry), and dressed with a sauce. Some filled, homemade pasta, *e.g., tortelloni,* are included in this family when they also are served with a sauce. To generalize, *pasta asciutta* is eaten with a fork. To generalize further, it is said in Italy that good *pasta asciutta* can be found only from Rome south. But that's a lot of *campanilismo* (fanatical devotion to one's own parish belltower).

2) *minestra:* soup in which either commercial or homemade pasta or rice and/or vegetables have been cooked. This particular

family has a sort of hierarchy: *minestr-one, minestr-a, minestr-ina* (thick and hearty, normal, thin). All are undeniably soupy and of course must be eaten with a spoon. A favorite *primo piatto* in colder weather, *minestra* is a common dish from North to South.

3) *risotto:* the dish in which rice is the star, not the supporting player, and is cooked so that it absorbs its cooking liquid, either water or broth. To eat it you can use either a spoon or a fork. It is said that a good *risotto* can be found only from Florence north, with Milan the *risotto* capital. But that's more *campanilismo.*

4) *gnocchi* (pronounced knee-oh-key): dumplings which, like *pasta asciutta,* are boiled in water, drained, and dressed with a sauce. Almost every Italian region has its own version of *gnocchi.*

5) *timballi:* casseroles whose main ingredient is either pasta or rice or vegetables or, sometimes, *polenta.* They are baked, served hot or cold, cut as a pie is cut, and are eaten with a fork. The head of this family is *lasagne,* a northern specialty.

6) *polenta:* Italy's famous cornmeal dish, which unfortunately has not had the exposure that pasta has had. Cooked in salted water (which it absorbs), it is served with a sauce. Classic *polenta* is poured onto a wooden serving board where it assumes the form of — or it is shaped as — a loaf. It is then cut into slices, which you eat with a fork. It is a staple of the mountainous North, where *polenta* can appear as a first course, a second course, and also as a dessert.

With all this said and done, take your choice of a *primo piatto.* But only one. Never, in an Italian meal, should two *primi piatti* be served. A *minestrone* followed by a dish of spaghetti is unthinkable. Even worse is spaghetti served as a side dish. Though we've seen it done, it's un-Italian.

PASTA ASCIUTTA / PASTA FOR SAUCES

Pasta comes in so many shapes and sizes that the mind boggles. Since all the varieties are made of the same basic ingredients, you would think that the whole list is purely an exercise in ingenuity and that size and shape shouldn't make much difference in the final dish. Well, they do. Each type of pasta is best suited for a particular dish because of its distinctive texture and the way it interacts with its sauce. In the recipes that follow we will indicate which pasta goes with which sauce. There is some leeway, naturally, but if you do make substitutions, choose a type of pasta closely resembling the one we recommend.

If macaroni (commercially produced and packaged pasta) can seemingly be found anywhere, the home is the only place you can find *pasta fatta in casa*, homemade pasta. It's made with all-purpose flour, water, and salt, or with the same flour, eggs, a pinch of salt, and no water at all, when it is called *pasta all'uovo*, egg pasta, a real gastronomical treat and more than worth its making. The big myth is that it's supposed to be hard to make, but once you've tried making it yourself, you'll know it's not difficult and is worth every single simple motion.

PASTA ALL'UOVO / EGG PASTA

HANDMADE: to make *pasta all'uovo* by hand all you need is: a clean flat surface (wood, marble, formica) about 24″ x 24″, a fork, a long (24″) rolling pin (a short pastry rolling pin is not efficient), and a sharp knife.

As a rule, 1 Italian serving of pasta calls for 1 medium egg, a scant ¾ cup of unbleached all-purpose flour, and a pinch of salt. This portion could be considered over-generous on the American

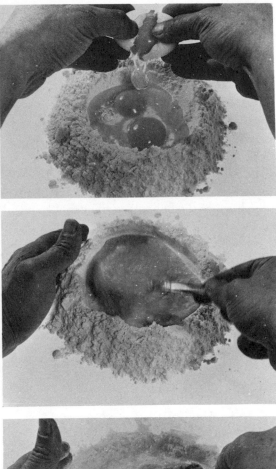

Make a mound of the flour on your counter or pastry board. Turn it into a crater and break the eggs into it.

Beat the eggs with a fork and let your free hand shore up the walls of the crater as well as spill some flour into the eggs.

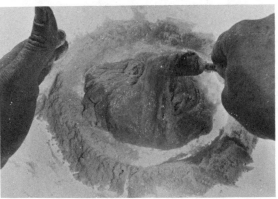

When most of the flour has been absorbed by the eggs the fork becomes useless.

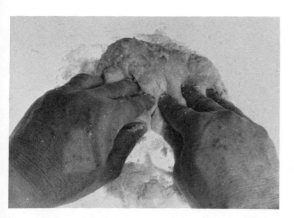

Work in the rest of your flour with your hands and then start kneading the dough.

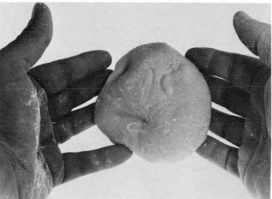

In 10 or 15 minutes of kneading, the dough is smooth and malleable.

Flour lightly the working surface and the rolling pin and roll out the pasta, working from the center out to the edges.

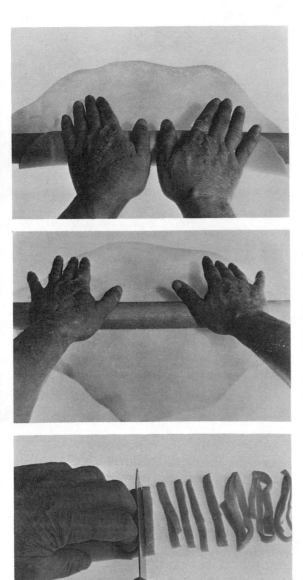

To reach the desired thickness
more quickly, flour the top side
of the pasta and let it roll itself
around the pin. Then roll away
from you with your hands
pressing down and sliding from
the center of the pin towards
the ends. Repeat the operation
from different angles until you
have a sheet of pasta of uniform
thickness.

Let the pasta dry for 10 to 15
minutes, flour it lightly, and
fold it over and over into a flat
roll about 4 inches wide. For
fettuccine, cut into ¼-inch-wide
strips, shake them out, and let
dry.

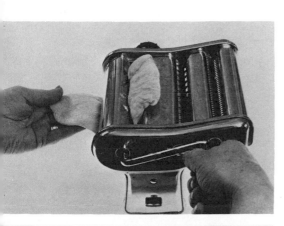

If using a pasta machine, break off a piece of dough and flatten it down to about the size of the palm of your hand. Flour it well and send it through the rollers at their widest gap.

Send the pasta through again and again, flouring it as needed, and reducing the gap between the rollers until the pasta has reached the desired thickness.

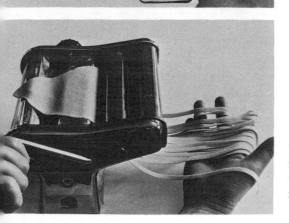

Let the pasta dry for 15 minutes, then send it through the cutting rollers of the machine.

table. So, we advise a 5-egg batch for 6 average American servings. As the number of servings increases, however, the number of eggs decreases: 7 eggs for 9 portions; 9 eggs for 12. With experience you'll be able to decide how many eggs for how many people. As a starting point, these amounts will produce 6 average servings:

> 3½ cups unbleached all-purpose flour (approximate)
> 5 medium eggs (at room temperature)
> ¼ teaspoon salt

If you are really new to the game and nervous, start with a smaller batch for 2 to 3 servings:

> 1½ cups unbleached all-purpose flour (approximate)
> 2 medium eggs (at room temperature)
> pinch of salt

We can only approximate the amount of flour (though our measurements are reasonably close) because of the many variables: the size and temperature of the eggs, the nature of the flour and the willingness of these two to get together, the heat of the room, the humidity in the air, the time and enthusiasm you put into the kneading. Given all these factors, you may have a bit of flour left over, but you can put it to good use in rolling out the dough. If, on the other hand, the eggs seem to want to absorb a little more flour, just give it to them.

Make a mound of the flour on the work surface. Make a hollow in the center of the mound large enough and deep enough to hold the eggs. It should look like a moon crater or, as it is poetically called in Italian, a fountain. Break the eggs into the hollow and add the salt. Shore up the walls of the crater to insure against spillage, and then take the fork in one hand and position the other to embrace the crater walls lovingly.

Beat the eggs with the fork as you would for an omelet. As you beat, the eggs will absorb flour. That's what you want and you can help the process by making some more flour spill over the edge of the crater into the thickening egg mixture (that loving embrace is not simply passive).

When the mixture has become quite thick, the fork is useless. But there is still flour to be incorporated, and so, put aside the fork, flour your hands, and with your fingers work as much of the rest of the flour into the egg mixture as you can.

When the eggs have absorbed as much flour as they possibly can, clean your hands and the working surface, and begin kneading. Everyone develops a kneading technique of his own but it is important that all the motions should compress and not stretch the dough. The main thing is to press down on the dough with the heels of your hands and roll the dough away from you. Then fold the dough in half, bring it back towards you, press and roll it away again. Flour your hands and surface as needed and keep on kneading until the dough loses all its stickiness and has become firm, smooth, and malleable.

If the dough tends to crack or obstinately refuses to become smooth, you have used too much flour. (If this should happen to a professional pasta-maker, he or she would be forced to retire without pension.) But you, as an amateur, can simply add a little water — very little — to the dough and knead until it is again smooth and moist. Depending on your energy and dexterity, total kneading time runs from 10 to 15 minutes. The pasta is golden, elastic, and ready for rolling. The working surface at this time is practically clean, but tidy it up completely and dust it again with flour.

Take a piece of dough (begin with one about the size of a tennis ball) and put it in the center of the working surface. Flatten it out as much as you can. Dust the rolling pin with flour and begin to roll. The rolling tends to squeeze moisture out of the dough and make it stick to the surface or pin, so flour both lightly as you continue rolling and as the dough turns into an almost round or oval sheet.

Once the dough has reached ¼-inch thickness, you can speed the rolling by wrapping the dough around the long pin. First, dust both pin and pasta with flour. Then position the pin on the edge of pasta closest to you. Wrap the edge of the pasta up over the pin, hold it there at the center of the pin, and roll away from you, letting the pasta wrap itself around the pin. Bring the pin with its roll of pasta back close to you and roll it away from you, pressing and sliding your hands toward the ends of the pin. Then unroll the pasta, turn it 90 degrees around, wrap the closest edge of the pasta round the pin, and roll as before. Keep going until you have a sheet of pasta of a uniform thickness, roughly the thickness of a dime.

When you have achieved the desired thickness, wrap the pasta around the rolling pin one more time, and unroll it onto a clean cloth. If you aren't going to cut the pasta right away, cover it with another clean cloth or plastic wrap.

MACHINE-MADE: having said all this, we must add that there is another way to produce homemade pasta — with a pasta machine. It gives rewarding results, especially if you lack space, and can save time as well, but not much once you have become adept with the long rolling pin. The pasta machine seems to be more widely stocked than ever before in both kitchenware and department stores. It is a buy for a lifetime and, considering the joy it gives, quite inexpensive. It does most of the kneading, all of the rolling, and some of the cutting. Yet the handmade pasta seems better than machine-made to us: no matter how perfect one is at rolling and cutting, handmade pasta gives little variations in thickness and size that add more character and texture to the final dish. It's the difference between the handcrafted and the machine-made.

When using a pasta machine, the ingredients and proportions are the same as for handmade pasta. The beginning is also the same: the crater, the eggs, the beating with a fork, the handworking until a manageable dough is obtained.

Cut a piece of unkneaded dough about the size of a tennis ball. Flatten it out, flour it on both sides, and pass it through the machine's rollers set at their widest opening. The first and perhaps the second rolling produce a raggedy affair. Don't be discouraged. Fold the dough over, flour it again, and give it another pass through the rollers. In a few passes, the pasta will have become even and smooth. Adjust the rollers to shrink the opening one notch and proceed as before. As the dough gets thinner, the strips of pasta get longer, and it is advisable to cut them into 10- to 15-inch lengths for easy handling. Also, as you progress toward the smallest gap between rollers, the dough ceases to be moist and needs less dusting with flour. The final pass through the rollers is only to give the thickness needed for the different cuts. And what you have now isn't dough anymore. It's a miracle, *pasta all'uovo!* The machine can cut it into various widths. Put the pasta strips to rest on clean cloths and, as with handmade pasta, cover with another cloth or plastic wrap if you are not going to cut it in the next 15 minutes.

CUTTING PASTA: Generally speaking, you dry pasta for *fettuccine* for about 15 minutes before cutting. Then dust the sheet with flour, fold it up in flat rolls about 4 inches wide, and slice into ribbons about ¼ inch wide. After a number of ribbons are cut, shake them out gently so that they unfold and put them back on the pasta cloth. They can be used at once or they can dry for up to 3 hours.

Pasta for *cannelloni, lasagne,* or *manicotti* should dry 15 minutes before cutting, and should sit no more than a half hour before cooking or it could become too brittle and break. *Cannelloni* are cut into rectangles about 4" x 5". *Lasagne* are rectangles about 4" x 6". They can be bigger, but if they are, it's harder to get them out of their cooking water. *Manicotti* are 4" x 4" squares.

For the smaller filled pasta, such as ravioli, *agnolotti,* or *tortelloni,* cut the pasta sheets into 2" x 2" squares or rounds 2 inches in diameter. The rule is to work as quickly as you can. Fill and fold and seal shut while the pasta is still moist enough to stick together when pressed. If it is not, dampen a finger and run it around the edges where the pasta is to be sealed.

Long or short, filled or unfilled, commercially produced or home-made, your pasta has to be properly cooked. It is the simplest of all operations, yet the most important. Poorly cooked or, worse yet, overcooked pasta not only wastes all the work you have put into it, from shopping to sauce, but also turns *pasta asciutta* into a mush hardly deserving its name.

A proper *pasta asciutta* is cooked *al dente,* a phrase that can be translated literally as "to the tooth" but is more reasonably interpreted as "that stage at which pasta is still biteable but tender, yet has a definite texture." Moreover, a pasta cooked *al dente* is a light, digestible affair; an overcooked pasta dish will sit in your stomach like wallpaper glue.

The timings you follow in cooking the pasta are all-important. There are two and they are closely related.

One is the actual length of time the pasta needs to be cooked, and this is exquisitely individual for each type of pasta. The cooking times given by manufacturers on packages should be taken as an indication, a ballpark figure. Even previous personal timings are not to be trusted, especially for homemade pasta.

Pasta, as soon as it hits the boiling water, becomes a living thing susceptible to the variables of a day: moisture, dryness, temperature, barometric pressure (or altitude above sea level). The only way to know when pasta is perfectly cooked is to put it to the test of your *dente,* tooth: *al dente,* just right to the feel as you bite. Pasta cooked *al dente* makes you appreciative and grateful for the centuries of ingenuity that have gone into the creation of a zillion shapes and sizes of pasta.

The second timing is when to put the pasta on to cook. Once cooked and drained, the pasta must be served and eaten immediately. If you delay, the pasta will overcook itself on the platter and then become cold. A cold pasta, even if *al dente,* is a dead pasta.

In Italy the most common battle cry is *"Butta giù!"* or "throw it down," and refers exclusively to the act of throwing down pasta into boiling water. It is a clarion call to alert everybody that in a few minutes the perfect dish of pasta will be on the table and everybody had better be there: delays are not allowed. The daily peak in the number of telephone calls in Italy is at lunch time, when the lines are overloaded with *"Butta giù!"* calls. It is the beginning of a national countdown. The callers are alerting the pasta cooks that they are leaving their place of business and that in so many minutes they will be home. Precisely in so many minutes, callers and pasta connect at the table, with not a minute to spare.

As soon as pasta is served, it has to be eaten. Many foreigners are frequently astounded at what they presume to be the Italian lack of table manners: people eat their pasta without waiting for the host's starting signal. They do not know that letting a steaming dish of pasta snuff itself out under one's eyes while waiting for everyone to be served is not etiquette but heresy. *Pasta asciutta* is never served at state ceremonies. Ferdinand, king of Naples and the two Sicilies (the kingdom of *Pasta asciutta*), never served pasta because, it is said, he knew that foreign dignitaries and their ladies did not appreciate it fully and it would have been a waste. After a banquet, the good King Ferdinand would sneak out and have a royal pasta feast in the royal kitchens with the royal cooks and maidens.

Now a few pointers for the simple operation of cooking pasta:

Choose a pot higher than it is wide, big enough to contain at least a quart of water per serving (*e.g.*, 6 quarts for 6 servings) but not less than 4 quarts for 3 servings or less.

Use a long wooden spoon or, better yet, a long wooden fork to stir the pasta while cooking.

Have a colander large enough to hold all the pasta you cook.

Cook in abundant, salted water, stir frequently, and check the stage of cooking by testing.

Drain thoroughly and serve right away.

THE TECHNIQUE: bring the water to a high boil, add a teaspoon of salt per quart of water. Add the pasta by handfuls — all the pasta at once certainly will startle the boiling water: it will take longer to come back to a boil and the pasta might stick in clumps. Once all the pasta is in, it takes but a few moments to become flexible. Make sure it is all immersed as quickly as possible by stirring with the wooden spoon or fork.

Cover the pot to hurry the return to a boil. One of the most heartening sounds in a kitchen is that of pasta boiling so hard it rattles the cover on the pot, letting out big puffs of steam. It may very well be that the tempo of the Neapolitan dance *tarantella* is based on this most cheerful rattle.

Once the pot boils, uncover it and stir the pasta. Homemade pasta surfaces at the first boil and, depending on its thickness, takes from 3 to 5 minutes to cook. Commercial pasta takes longer, between 6 and 12 minutes depending on size, even 15 to 17 minutes for big macaroni.

As soon as the cooking pasta is limp and willing to wrap itself around the wooden fork, fish out a piece. Blow on it and as soon as temperature permits, bite on it. If the pasta has a barely crisp core to it, it has to cook only another minute or so. Keep testing and you will know when the *al dente* stage has arrived: the pasta is cooked throughout and yet there is a suspicion of a core in it. Drain it. Put in serving bowl. Sauce over. Mix. Serve. Eat. Ah!

PASTA ASCIUTTA: IL SUGO /
SAUCES FOR PASTA

By the time you've made or selected your pasta, you should have chosen your sauce. Or vice-versa, since pasta and sauce are so interrelated that they become one. To help in that choice we've divided the dishes into four groups, with an indication of the type of pasta best suited to or most commonly used with each sauce. The fourth group consists of sauces made with fish or which use anchovies for flavoring. Like the Italian cook, let the market, the mood, the weather, and the season, as well as your own time and money, influence your choice.

These cheese and/or vegetable sauces use fresh seasonal ingredients. They're easy to make and take barely more time to cook than is necessary to boil the pasta that goes with them.

CONCHIGLIE A FUNGHETTO /
SHELL PASTA WITH MUSHROOM-STYLE SAUCE

"*A funghetto*" is a general term used to describe vegetables cut and cooked as if they were mushrooms. In this case eggplant and zucchini are cooked like — and join — the real thing: mushrooms.

SAUCE
2 small eggplants
2 small zucchini
¾ pound mushrooms
3 tablespoons chopped fresh parsley, including some stem
2 garlic cloves
½ cup olive oil
¾ teaspoon oregano
1½ teaspoons salt, or to taste

PASTA
6 quarts water
6 teaspoons salt
1 pound shell pasta

Halve lengthwise and salt the eggplants (pages 7–9). When they have drained sufficiently, cut them crosswise into thin, half-moon slices. Wash the zucchini and slice them like the eggplants. Clean and slice the mushrooms.

Finely chop the parsley with the garlic, and sauté in olive oil in a big pot over medium heat until limp. Add the sliced eggplant and continue cooking 5 minutes. Add the zucchini and mushroom slices, stir well, sprinkle with oregano, stir again, cover, and continue cooking 10 minutes or until the vegetables are tender but still slightly crisp. They shouldn't be mushy. Taste for salt and add if necessary.

While the vegetables are cooking, cook and drain the pasta (pages 56–58). Add it to the vegetables. Stir well and serve. For 6.

PAPARELE E BISI / FETTUCCINE WITH PEAS

This is a delicate, satisfying dish, traditionally served for the feast of San Zeno, Patron Saint of Verona. (Can you imagine how much better off Romeo and Juliet would have been if they'd settled for a dish of *paparele* instead of a swig from that vial?) The same sauce can be used with small *rigatoni,* spaghetti, or the pasta of your choice, but with homemade *fettuccine,* which are called *paparele* in Verona, it is a dish fit for a saint.

SAUCE
1½ pounds fresh peas, or 1½ 10-ounce packages frozen tiny peas
1 medium onion
3 tablespoons chopped fresh parsley
6 tablespoons unsalted butter
4 tablespoons olive oil
1 teaspoon salt
freshly ground pepper
2 teaspoons sugar
4 to 5 tablespoons grated Parmesan cheese

PASTA
6 quarts water
6 teaspoons salt
1 5-egg batch *Pasta all'uovo* (pages 47–55) cut for *fettuccine,* or 1¼ pounds egg noodles

If using frozen peas, thaw them at room temperature and spread them out on absorbent paper to dry a bit before they go into the pan.

Finely chop the onion and parsley, and sauté them in 2 tablespoons of the butter and all of the olive oil in a frying pan or saucepan large enough so that when the peas are added they can cook in one layer. When the onion is wilted and translucent, add the peas, salt, and a couple of twists of pepper. Bring to a boil. Add the sugar, lower the heat to a gentle simmer, cover the pan when the contents boil, and cook for 15 or 20 minutes, or until the peas are tender but not overcooked. Frozen peas take about half as much time to cook as fresh ones. Stir occasionally and make sure there is enough liquid in the pan. If not, add 1 or 2 tablespoons of warm water to guarantee a sauce.

Cook and drain the *paparele* (pages 56–58). Put the remaining butter into a warm serving bowl, pour the hot *paparele* on top of it, and add the peas and their sauce. Mix well, sprinkle with the Parmesan cheese, and toss again so that the cheese and sauce blend. Serve immediately. For 6.

PENNE AL CAVOLFIORE /
MACARONI WITH CAULIFLOWER

The cauliflower in this case isn't really made into a sauce: it is cooked along with the pasta (*ziti, mostaccioli, penne,* or big elbow macaroni are recommended) and is then dressed with flavored olive oil.

    1 cauliflower
    6 quarts water
    6 teaspoons salt
    1 pound *ziti* or *mostaccioli*
    4 garlic cloves
    1 red pepper pod, seeded
    ½ cup olive oil
    freshly ground pepper

1 tablespoon chopped fresh parsley
3 to 4 tablespoons grated Romano cheese (optional)

Break the cauliflower into flowerets, discarding the core. Bring
the water to a boil, salt it, and add the flowerets. When the water
comes back to a boil, add the pasta, and cook at a high boil until
it is *al dente.*

Meanwhile, sauté the garlic and red pepper in the olive oil
until the garlic is golden and the pepper dark brown. Then remove and discard them.

Drain the pasta and cauliflower, put them into a warm serving
bowl, add the flavored olive oil, and toss gently. Add freshly
ground pepper and the parsley. Toss again and serve, passing the
Romano cheese around for those who wish it. For 6.

RIGATONI STRACINATI IN PADELLA /
RIGATONI WITH BASIL-AND-PARSLEY SAUCE

Stracinati in padella is dialect for "dragged around in a pan." In
culinary terms this phrase means "sautéed quickly over high
heat," which goes to prove that even in the number of words in
its name *rigatoni stracinati* is an economical dish. It is also a quick
and delightful summer dish to serve when the flavor of fresh
herbs is at its height.

SAUCE
1 cup loosely packed fresh basil leaves
1 cup loosely packed fresh parsley leaves
4 tablespoons olive oil
4 tablespoons unsalted butter
1 teaspoon salt
freshly ground pepper
4 to 5 tablespoons grated Parmesan cheese

PASTA
6 quarts water

6 teaspoons salt
1¼ pounds *rigatoni*

Put the *rigatoni* on to cook (pages 56–58).

While it is cooking, chop the basil and parsley well. Heat the oil and butter in a pot large enough to hold the *rigatoni* when cooked. Add the chopped herbs, salt, and pepper. Stir and cook over low heat for a minute or two.

When the *rigatoni* are cooked and drained, add them to the herb-flavored oil. Raise the heat, stir well, and sprinkle with the Parmesan cheese. Keep stirring until everything is well mixed. Serve immediately. For 6.

SPAGHETTI AI FUNGHI /
SPAGHETTI WITH MUSHROOMS

SAUCE
1 pound large mushrooms, preferably golden
½ cup olive oil
2 tablespoons unsalted butter
1½ teaspoons salt, or to taste
freshly ground pepper
3 tablespoons chopped fresh parsley
juice of ½ lemon

PASTA
6 quarts water
6 teaspoons salt
1¼ pounds spaghetti

Clean the mushrooms and cut them into thin slices. Put 6 table-spoons of the olive oil and the butter into a large frying pan. Add the sliced mushrooms and sauté briefly, salting them and adding the pepper as they cook. As soon as the mushrooms begin to wilt, add the parsley, stir and cook for a minute, add the lemon juice, and stir and cook for another minute.

Cook and drain the pasta (pages 56–58), put in a warm serving bowl, and dress with the mushrooms. Add the remaining olive oil, toss, and serve. Additional lemon juice may be added to individual taste. For 6.

SPAGHETTI ALLA CARBONARA DI MAGRO /
MEATLESS SPAGHETTI, CHARCOAL MAKERS' STYLE

SAUCE
3 eggs
4 tablespoons olive oil
4 tablespoons milk
½ cup grated Parmesan cheese
½ cup grated Swiss cheese
½ teaspoon salt
freshly ground pepper

PASTA
6 quarts water
6 teaspoons salt
1¼ pounds spaghetti

Put the spaghetti on to cook in boiling, salted water (pages 56–58).

Beat the eggs in a shallow, wide serving bowl and mix in all the other sauce ingredients.

When the pasta is *al dente,* drain well, and put it on top of the beaten eggs. Toss immediately and thoroughly so that the heat of the pasta cooks the eggs. Add a generous amount of freshly ground pepper to taste. Serve immediately. For 6.

SPAGHETTI CON LE ZUCCHINE /
SPAGHETTI WITH ZUCCHINI

SAUCE
5 medium zucchini
1 garlic clove
½ cup olive oil
1 teaspoon salt, or to taste
freshly ground pepper

PASTA
6 quarts water
6 teaspoons salt
1¼ pounds spaghetti

Cut both ends off the zucchini and slice into thin rounds.

Sauté the garlic in the olive oil in a big frying pan over medium heat until golden. Remove the garlic and fry the zucchini in the flavored oil, putting in as many slices as will comfortably fit in a single layer. When one layer is golden brown on both sides remove it to a bowl and fry another. When all are done, sprinkle with salt and pepper, the latter generously.

Cook and drain the pasta (pages 56–58). Put it on a warm serving platter, cover with the zucchini rounds, and pour on the oil they were cooked in. Toss gently, but don't hope to get the zucchini perfectly distributed: they tend to sink to the bottom and must be distributed evenly over the individual portions. For 6.

TAGLIATELLE CON BIETA E FUNGHI /
EGG NOODLES WITH SWISS CHARD AND MUSHROOMS

SAUCE
1 pound Swiss chard

¼ pound fresh mushrooms
6 tablespoons unsalted butter
salt to taste
3 tablespoons olive oil
6 tablespoons grated Parmesan cheese

PASTA
6 quarts water
6 teaspoons salt
1 5-egg batch *Pasta all'uovo* (pages 47–55), or 1¼ pounds
egg noodles

Wash the chard thoroughly, cut the leaves from the stems. Bring a big pot of water to boil, salt it, put in the stems, and when the water has returned to a boil add the leaves. When the stems are tender, drain the chard, pressing it down in the colander with a plate. When it's cool enough to handle, squeeze out any remaining water with your hands. Chop the cooked chard well.

Wash the mushrooms and cut them into thin slices. Melt the butter in a big frying pan and sauté the mushrooms 5 minutes or until just limp. Add salt, the chard, and the olive oil, and stir well. Continue cooking about 3 minutes, or until the chard is heated through. Taste for salt and add some if necessary.

Cook and drain the pasta (pages 56–58), and put it into a shallow, wide, and warm serving dish. Dress with the mushrooms and chard, sprinkle with the Parmesan cheese, toss well and serve. For 6.

VERMICELLI ALLA BELLA GINA /
VERMICELLI WITH TRUFFLES AND PEAS

Here is what we consider an incredibly delicious sauce. True, truffles are a rare item. Hence we recommend the best ingredients, either homemade egg pasta or top quality commercial *ver-*

micelli, the tiniest fresh or frozen peas, and a piece of good Parmesan cheese to be grated at the last minute so as not to lose any of its flavor.

SAUCE

1 10-ounce package frozen tiny peas, or 1 pound fresh
6 tablespoons unsalted butter
2 or 3 truffles, sliced paper thin
½ teaspoon freshly ground pepper
½ cup freshly grated Parmesan cheese

PASTA

6 quarts water
6 teaspoons salt
1¼ pounds *vermicelli*
1 5-egg batch *Pasta all'uovo* (pages 47–55) cut in narrow *fettuccine*, or 1¼ pounds *vermicelli*

Cook the frozen peas a minute in boiling salted water. If using fresh peas, be sure they are tiny also, and extend the cooking time to about 4 minutes, or until just tender.

Melt the butter in a medium-sized saucepan over low heat. Add the sliced truffles, pepper, and peas. Continue cooking over low heat about 5 minutes to flavor the butter.

Cook the *vermicelli* and drain thoroughly (pages 56–58), and put it onto a warm serving platter. Add the pea-truffle sauce, toss gently, and serve with the Parmesan cheese. For 6.

Sauces: Second Group

This family is a variation on the first group, in that it includes many of the same vegetables but with the *allegro* touch of the tomato. It may take a bit more time to prepare some of these dishes, but not enough to put you off your stride.

BUCATINI ALLA CARRETTIERA /
MACARONI, CART DRIVERS' STYLE

Until the total domination of the automobile, commerce in Italy moved on the wheels of the *carretti,* or carts, drawn by horses, oxen, mules, or lonely donkeys. *Carrettieri* were their drivers, the truckers of old, the undisputed masters of the road, known for their frequent, sudden, and rustic appetites. This recipe is the southern version, from Sicily, and on pages 78–79 is a second version from Lazio-Campania.

SAUCE

5 or 6 (2 pounds) very ripe fresh salad tomatoes
2 garlic cloves
10 fresh basil leaves
1½ teaspoons salt
freshly ground pepper
6 tablespoons olive oil

PASTA

6 quarts water
6 teaspoons salt
1¼ pounds thin macaroni (*bucatini* or *perciatelli*)

Peel the tomatoes, cut them into small chunks, and put them into the pasta serving dish. Chop together the garlic and basil, and add them to the tomatoes. Add the salt, freshly ground pepper in abundance (10 twists of the mill is a good amount), and the olive oil. Stir, and marinate for 1 hour.

Cook the pasta (pages 56–58) and drain especially well, shaking the colander to get out all the water before putting the pasta on top of the uncooked sauce. Toss and serve. For 6.

PASTASCIUTTA DI MAGRO /
PASTA WITH TOMATO-AND-ONION SAUCE

SAUCE

1 large onion or 2 small
1 large garlic clove or 2 small
6 tablespoons chopped fresh parsley
6 tablespoons olive oil
2½ to 3 cups (1½ pounds) very ripe plum tomatoes
1½ teaspoons salt, or to taste
3 to 4 tablespoons grated Parmesan cheese

PASTA

6 quarts water
6 teaspoons salt
1¼ pounds spaghetti

Chop together the onion, garlic, and parsley, and sauté in the olive oil until the onion bits are barely golden. Peel the tomatoes, cut them in half, scoop out the seeds into a sieve so that you can strain and save any juice. Cut the tomatoes into chunks, and add them and any juice to the flavored olive oil. Bring the pan to a boil, lower the heat, and cover the pan. Simmer for 20 minutes, stirring occasionally. Uncover the pan and continue simmering for another 5 to 10 minutes, or until the sauce has condensed, its color deepened. Add the salt, stir, taste, and adjust the seasoning if necessary.

Cook and drain the pasta (pages 56–58). Place it in a warm serving dish, dress with the sauce, toss gently, sprinkle with cheese, and serve. For 6.

PASTA E MELANZANE FRITTE/
SPAGHETTI WITH FRIED EGGPLANT

SAUCE
2 medium (1¼ pounds) eggplants
vegetable oil for frying
2 garlic cloves
4 tablespoons olive oil
3 cups peeled plum tomatoes
10 fresh basil leaves
1½ teaspoons salt
freshly ground pepper
8 tablespoons crumbled cheese (salted *ricotta* or *feta*)

PASTA
6 quarts water
6 teaspoons salt
1¼ pounds spaghetti

Slice the eggplants lengthwise into ¼-inch slices and prepare as usual (pages 7–9). Then cut them into thin strips 2 inches long. Bring the vegetable oil to high heat and fry the eggplant strips a few at a time until crisp and golden. Remove with a slotted spoon and drain on absorbent paper. Continue until all the strips have been fried.

Cut the garlic cloves into halves and sauté them in the olive oil in a large frying pan until golden. Discard the cloves.

Cut the tomatoes into chunks and add them to the olive oil after you have let it cool a bit in order to avoid great splattering. Chop the basil coarsely and add to the simmering sauce. Add the salt and 4 or 5 twists of pepper from the mill. Continue to simmer for about 20 minutes or until condensed, darker in color, and of sauce consistency. Taste for salt and add some if necessary.

Cook and drain the pasta (pages 56–58), and place it in a warm serving dish, either a deep platter or shallow, wide bowl. Dress with the tomato sauce and toss well. Distribute the eggplant

strips on top. Sprinkle on the crumbled cheese, toss gently, and
serve immediately. For 6.

PENNE E CAVOLFIORI AL SUGO /
MACARONI AND CAULIFLOWER WITH
TOMATO SAUCE

Cauliflower and macaroni are cooked together and married to
a sauce of fresh or canned tomatoes.

SAUCE
1 small onion
3 garlic cloves
½ cup olive oil
2 cups peeled plum tomatoes, cut in chunks
1 teaspoon salt, or to taste
3 tablespoons chopped fresh parsley
4 tablespoons grated Romano cheese

PASTA
7 quarts water
7 teaspoons salt
1 cauliflower
1 pound macaroni (*penne, mostaccioli,* or *ziti*)

Finely chop the onion and garlic together and sauté them in a
large frying pan over medium heat until limp and golden. Add
the cut-up tomatoes to the flavored olive oil. Bring to a lively
boil and then lower the heat to simmer. Add salt and, stirring
occasionally, cook about 20 minutes, or until reduced in liquid and
deepened in color. Add the parsley, stir, and remove from heat.

Break the cauliflower into flowerets. Bring the water to a boil,
salt it, and add the cauliflower. When the water is back to a boil,
add the pasta, cook until *al dente,* and drain thoroughly.

Put the pasta and cauliflower into a large serving bowl which has been warmed, add the tomato sauce, and toss gently. Sprinkle with Romano cheese and serve. For 6.

RIGATONI CON ASPARAGI /
RIGATONI WITH ASPARAGUS, BEATEN EGGS, AND TOMATOES

This almost might be called a vegetarian's *pasta alla carbonara,* whereas *Spaghetti alla carbonara di magro* (page 64) is the cheese lover's. The common denominator in the three recipes is of course beaten eggs.

SAUCE
½ cup olive oil
2 garlic cloves
1 cup peeled plum tomatoes
½ teaspoon salt
1 pound fresh asparagus
2 eggs
4 tablespoons grated Romano cheese
freshly ground pepper

PASTA
6 quarts water
6 teaspoons salt
1 pound *rigatoni* or similar macaroni

Sauté the garlic in the olive oil in a large frying pan over medium heat until golden and then discard the cloves. Mash the tomatoes with a fork and add them to the flavored oil. Add the salt and cook, stirring from time to time, for 15 minutes, or until reduced and darkened in color.

Break off and discard the tough bottoms of the asparagus, and cut the rest into bite-sized lengths. Cook in abundant, boiling, salted water until tender but still slightly crisp. Drain thoroughly.

Beat the eggs right in the serving bowl or platter. Add the

cooked, cooled asparagus, abundant ground pepper, and the cheese.

Cook and drain the pasta (pages 56–58), and add immediately to the asparagus and eggs. Toss gently, letting the heat of the pasta cook the eggs. Add the tomato sauce, toss again, and serve. For 6.

RIGATONI CON SUGO MAGRO DI RICOTTA /
RIGATONI WITH TOMATO-AND-RICOTTA SAUCE

SAUCE
½ small carrot
1 small onion
1 celery stalk
3 parsley sprigs
4 tablespoons olive oil or unsalted butter
2 cups peeled plum tomatoes, cut in chunks
½ teaspoon salt, or to taste
3 basil leaves
½ pound *ricotta*
3 to 4 tablespoons grated Parmesan cheese, minimum

PASTA
6 quarts water
6 teaspoons salt
1¼ pounds *rigatoni*

Chop the carrot, onion, celery, and parsley to a paste and sauté in the oil (or butter) over medium heat about 8 minutes, or until cooked and golden.

Add the tomatoes to the flavored oil. Add the salt and simmer for 10 minutes. Tear the basil leaves into pieces and add them to the sauce. Cook another 5 minutes, or until reduced to a good sauce consistency. Cool a bit and then mix in the *ricotta* thoroughly.

Cook and drain the pasta (pages 56–58). Put in a warm serving dish and dress with the *ricotta* sauce. Serve immediately with Parmesan cheese to be added as desired. For 6.

SPAGHETTI ALLA SPOLETINA /
SPAGHETTI WITH TRUFFLES

SAUCE
⅓ cup olive oil
1 garlic clove
1 salted anchovy, or 2 canned fillets
¼ cup tomato paste, diluted in ½ cup warm water
2 or 3 black truffles
1 tablespoon chopped fresh parsley

PASTA
6 quarts water
6 teaspoons salt
1¼ pounds thin spaghetti

If using a salted anchovy, fillet it (page 15); if using canned fillets, drain them. Chop finely the anchovy fillets and cook gently with the garlic in the olive oil over low heat until the anchovies have disintegrated and the garlic is golden. Discard the cloves and cool the oil a bit. Add the diluted tomato paste to the cooled oil. Stirring constantly, bring the mixture to a low boil, and cook until the oil and tomato blend into a sauce.

Mince the truffles as finely as possible and add them, along with the parsley, to the tomatoes. Simmer another 5 minutes. Taste for salt and add some if necessary. If using canned truffles, also add their canning liquid.

Cook and drain the pasta (pages 56–58) and put it on a warm, deep serving platter. Add the truffle sauce, toss well, and serve immediately. For 6.

SPAGHETTI CON LE PUNTE D'ASPARAGI /
SPAGHETTI WITH ASPARAGUS-AND-TOMATO SAUCE

SAUCE

1½ pounds fresh asparagus, or 2 10-ounce packages frozen cut
    asparagus
½ cup olive oil
1 teaspoon salt, or to taste
2 cups peeled and mashed plum tomatoes, preferably fresh
freshly ground pepper

PASTA

6 quarts water
6 teaspoons salt
1¼ pounds spaghetti

If using fresh asparagus, break off the root end of the asparagus
stems and cut the edible part into bite-sized pieces. Wash and pat
dry with paper towels. If using frozen, defrost and pat dry.

Put the asparagus and the olive oil into a big frying pan over
medium heat and sauté for 2 minutes. Add the salt, stir, and add
the mashed plum tomatoes. Cook uncovered over medium heat
15 to 20 minutes.

Cook and drain the pasta (pages 56–58), and put on a warm,
deep platter. Add the asparagus sauce, toss gently, and serve.
For 6.

VERMICELLI ALLA SAMMARTINESE /
VERMICELLI WITH SWEET PEPPERS

SAUCE

2 garlic cloves
6 tablespoons olive oil
2 cups peeled plum tomatoes, cut in chunks
3 or 4 large (approximately 1½ pounds) sweet peppers (red,
    green, or yellow)
2 tablespoons grated Romano cheese

PASTA
6 quarts water
6 teaspoons salt
1¼ pounds *vermicelli* or thin spaghetti

Sauté the garlic in the olive oil in a big frying pan over medium heat until golden and then discard the cloves. Cool the oil a bit and add the tomatoes. Bring to a boil, lower the heat, and simmer, stirring occasionally.

Remove the stems and cores of the peppers and cut them into strips. Add to the simmering sauce and continue cooking for about 20 minutes, or until the peppers are tender and the sauce has condensed a bit.

Mix in the cheese.

Cook and drain the pasta (pages 56–58), put it on a warm serving dish, and cover with sauce. Toss well. Serve with additional cheese to individual taste. For 6.

VERMICELLI ALLA SIRACUSANA /
VERMICELLI IN THE STYLE OF SYRACUSE

Simply translating the name of this pasta dish doesn't tell you much at all, but a cook of Syracuse in Sicily would need no further description of this sauce made of eggplant, sweet yellow peppers, plum tomatoes, flavored with herbs, and cooked only long enough to tenderize and not so long as to lose color. The sauce is most frequently paired with *vermicelli*, but if you're not a traditionalist, it's also good with rice.

SAUCE
1 medium eggplant
1 large sweet yellow pepper
½ cup olive oil
1 garlic clove
2 cups peeled plum tomatoes, cut in chunks

12 pitted Sicilian black olives (packed in brine, not dried)
3 or 4 fresh basil leaves
1 tablespoon capers
salt to taste
3 or 4 tablespoons grated Romano cheese, or to taste

PASTA
6 quarts water
6 teaspoons salt
1¼ pounds *vermicelli*

Cut the eggplant in half lengthwise, and prepare as usual (pages 7–9). After scraping off the salt, cut the eggplant into small cubes.

Roast the pepper (page 36). Remove its charred skin, core it, and cut it into thin strips.

Heat the olive oil in a big frying pan over medium heat. Add the garlic and sauté until golden, then discard it. Add the cubed eggplant and cook for 5 minutes, or until the eggplant is a bit limp and golden. Add the tomatoes, raise the heat to a boil, and then lower to a simmer.

Chop the olives coarsely with the basil and capers. (If using salted capers, wash them thoroughly.) Add these flavorings to the tomato sauce, and continue simmering for 15 minutes. After 7 or 8 minutes, taste for salt (the olives and the capers have added some) and add more if necessary.

Cook and drain the pasta (pages 56–58), and put in a warm serving bowl. Add the sauce, toss gently, sprinkle with the cheese, and serve. For 6.

Sauces: Third Group

These herb and/or nut sauces are just different enough from the others to deserve a space apart.

LINGUINE ALLA GENOVESE COL PESTO /
LINGUINE, GENOESE STYLE (WITH PESTO)

SAUCE
6 tablespoons *Pesto* (pages 21–22)

PASTA
6 quarts water
3 (1 pound) medium potatoes
6 teaspoons salt
1¼ pounds *linguine*
1 10-ounce package French-cut frozen green beans, or ¾
    pound tiny, fresh

While the pasta water is coming to a boil, peel the potatoes and cut them into bite-sized cubes. When the water boils, salt it, add the potatoes, and cook for 5 minutes. Add the beans and when the water comes back to a boil, add the *linguine.*

When the pasta is *al dente,* drain it quickly and thoroughly but try to save some of the pasta water (either by scooping off ½ cup before draining or by putting the colander back over the pasta pot as it drains).

Once the pasta and vegetables are in a warm serving dish, add the *pesto* and mix well. Add enough of the saved pasta water to dilute the *pesto* so that it coats the pasta nicely all over. Serve immediately. For 6.

SPAGHETTI ALLA CARRETTIERA /
SPAGHETTI, CART DRIVERS' STYLE

SAUCE
3 or 4 garlic cloves
½ cup olive oil
1 large onion
¼ cup chopped fresh parsley

½ teaspoon oregano
½ teaspoon salt, or to taste
freshly ground pepper
5 tablespoons unseasoned bread crumbs

PASTA
6 quarts water
6 teaspoons salt
1¼ pounds spaghetti

Sauté the garlic in all but 2 tablespoons of the olive oil, and then discard when the cloves are golden.

Sliver the onions and sauté in the flavored olive oil until wilted. Add the parsley with the oregano. Continue cooking until the onion slivers are barely golden.

Toast the bread crumbs in a small saucepan with the remaining olive oil until they are golden brown.

Cook and drain the pasta (pages 56–58) and put it in a warm serving dish. Dress with the onion sauce and the toasted bread crumbs, toss gently, and serve. For 6.

TAGLIATELLE CON LE NOCI /
EGG NOODLES WITH WALNUT SAUCE

Tagliatelle is a regional name for narrow *fettuccine,* and the two are usually interchangeable.

SAUCE
1 4¼-ounce package chopped walnuts
2 tablespoons olive oil
salt
freshly ground pepper
¼ pound unsalted butter
3 tablespoons tomato paste, diluted in 1 cup warm water
6 tablespoons grated Parmesan cheese

6 quarts water

6 teaspoons salt

1 5-egg batch *Pasta all'uovo* (pages 47–55) cut in ¼-inch strips

Pound the walnuts in a mortar and then toast them in a small pan with the olive oil, a pinch of salt, and a few twists of pepper. When the nuts are well toasted, add the butter and the diluted tomato paste. Bring to a boil, lower the heat, and simmer about 20 minutes, or until a sauce consistency is achieved.

Cook and drain the pasta (pages 56–58). Put it onto a warm serving platter or into a wide shallow bowl, also warm. Add the sauce, toss well and serve with the Parmesan cheese. For 6.

Sauces: Fourth Group

Except for the arc of the Alps, Italy is surrounded by seas. They are celebrated here by these fish sauces starring anchovies, mussels, squid, and tuna, with herb seasonings and/or tomatoes.

BUCATINI COLL'ACCIUGHE/
MACARONI WITH TOMATO-AND-ANCHOVY SAUCE

SAUCE

6 garlic cloves

⅔ cup olive oil

10 large salted anchovies

3 cups peeled plum tomatoes

5 tablespoons chopped fresh parsley

½ cup coarse unseasoned bread crumbs

PASTA

6 quarts water

6 teaspoons salt
1¼ pounds thin macaroni (*bucatini* or *perciatelli*)

Sauté the garlic in the olive oil (reserving 1 tablespoon) in a medium-sized saucepan until golden. Then discard the cloves, and remove the pan from the heat for a moment or two to cool.

Clean the anchovies under running water (page 15), pat dry with absorbent paper, and add to the cooled, seasoned olive oil. Bring to a simmer and cook until the anchovies have disintegrated.

Pass the tomatoes through a sieve or food mill, add them to the anchovies, and continue simmering the sauce for 15 minutes. Taste for salt, add some if necessary.

Toast the bread crumbs in a frying pan with the reserved tablespoon of olive oil until golden brown.

Cook and drain the pasta (pages 56–58) and put it into a warm serving dish. Dress with the sauce, sprinkle with the chopped parsley and the toasted bread crumbs, and serve immediately. For 6.

BUCATINI CON LE SARDE ALLA SICILIANA /
MACARONI WITH FRESH SARDINES, SICILIAN STYLE

You should go out of your way to find fresh sardines for this dish, but do not pass it up if you have only quick-frozen ones. The pasta, garnished with the fish, raisins, and pine nuts, is a Sicilian dish with an Arabian flavor.

SAUCE
12 or 14 (2 pounds) large sardines, fresh or frozen
6 tablespoons olive oil
½ cup (approximate) coarse unseasoned bread crumbs
1½ garlic cloves
1 large onion
1 packet (.005 ounce) Italian saffron

½ cup golden raisins
3 tablespoons pine nuts

6 quarts water
2 tablespoons fennel seeds
6 teaspoons salt
1¼ pounds thin macaroni (*bucatini* or *perciatelli*)

If you have to use frozen sardines, thaw them at room temperature for an hour or so.

Clean the fish by scaling them carefully and removing the innards; cut off the heads and tails and discard them. Poach the fish in gently boiling salted water for 3 minutes. Remove the sardines with a slotted spoon and, when cool enough to handle, bone them. Peel off the skin.

Put 1½ tablespoons of the olive oil into a small frying pan and toast the bread crumbs until golden brown.

Put the remaining oil into a large frying pan, add the garlic, sauté until golden, and then discard it. Finely chop the onion and sauté it in the flavored oil until barely golden.

Moisten the saffron with 1 tablespoon of warm water. Add the sardines, raisins, and saffron water to the onions and cook for 5 minutes. Stir in 2 tablespoons of the toasted bread crumbs at the last minute.

Wrap the fennel seeds in cheesecloth. Bring the water to a boil, add the fennel seeds, salt, and the pasta. Stir, return to a boil, and cook the pasta until *al dente*. Drain well, remove the fennel, and put the pasta onto a warm, deep serving platter. Add the sardines with their sauce. Toss very gently, sprinkle with the last of the bread crumbs, and serve. For 6.

BUCATINI DELLA VIGILIA DI NATALE /
CHRISTMAS EVE MACARONI

SAUCE
5 large salted anchovies, or 8 to 10 canned fillets
⅔ cup olive oil
8 pitted Sicilian black olives (packed in brine, not dried)
2 tablespoons capers
freshly ground pepper
1 cup unseasoned bread crumbs

PASTA
6 quarts water
6 teaspoons salt
1¼ pounds thin macaroni (*bucatini* or *perciatelli*)

If using salted anchovies, fillet them (page 15). If using the canned fillets, just drain off the oil.

Mince the anchovies and put them in a saucepan with all but 1 tablespoon of oil. Cook over low heat until the anchovies have disintegrated.

Mince together the olives and capers. Add to the simmering anchovies.

Put the remaining olive oil into a frying pan, add the bread crumbs, and toast them over medium heat until golden brown.

Cook and drain the pasta (pages 56–58). Shake the colander to make sure all the water runs out of the pasta.

Spread the pasta on a warm, deep serving platter, sprinkle with half the bread crumbs, toss well, and add the anchovy mixture. Toss again. Add coarsely ground pepper. Serve the remaining bread crumbs as you would grated cheese. For 6.

SPAGHETTI AI PISELLI E SEPPIE /
SPAGHETTI WITH PEAS AND SQUID

This is an enriched version of the preceding recipe. It uses the same ingredients plus tiny peas for varied taste and color. It, too, can be used on spaghetti, with boiled rice, or alone, with slices of fresh Italian bread, as a second course.

    2 pounds squid, fresh or frozen
    2 garlic cloves
    ⅓ cup olive oil
    1 large onion
    3 tablespoons tomato paste, diluted in ½ cup warm water
    4 fresh basil leaves
    1 teaspoon salt
    ½ teaspoon sugar
    1 10-ounce package frozen tiny peas

Proceed exactly as in the preceding recipe. After the squid has simmered for 10 minutes, add the peas, raise the heat until the sauce comes back to a boil, then lower to simmer and continue cooking another 5 to 10 minutes. For 6.

SPAGHETTI AL SUGO DI COZZE /
SPAGHETTI WITH MUSSEL SAUCE

SAUCE
    2 pounds mussels
    1 medium onion
    1 garlic clove
    3 tablespoons chopped fresh parsley
    4 fresh basil leaves
    4 tablespoons olive oil
    1 tablespoon unsalted butter
    6 peeled plum tomatoes, chopped

½ cup very dry wine, red or white
½ teaspoon salt, or to taste

PASTA
6 quarts water
6 teaspoons salt
1¼ pounds spaghetti

Clean the mussels (page 151). Put enough water to cover the bottom into a pot big enough to hold the mussels. Bring to a boil over high heat, add the mussels, cover, and cook about 5 minutes, or until the mussels have been steamed open. Put aside to cool.

Chop together the onion, garlic, parsley, and basil, and sauté them in the olive oil and butter until the leaves have darkened and the bits of onion are golden. Add the chopped tomatoes and wine, stir, bring to a boil, and then lower the heat and simmer for about 15 minutes.

While the sauce is simmering, take the mussels out of their shells, holding them over the pot in order to save all their juice. Strain the juice through a sieve lined with cheesecloth. Chop the mussels coarsely. Once the sauce has boiled down and is quite reduced, add the mussels and ½ cup of the strained juice. Stir and simmer slowly for another 5 to 10 minutes, or until the sauce is reasonably thick again. Taste for salt.

Cook and drain the spaghetti (pages 56–58), and put it into a warm serving dish. Pour the sauce on top, toss, and serve. For 6.

SPAGHETTI AL SUGO DI SEPPIE I /
SPAGHETTI WITH SQUID SAUCE I

Here is a jack of all trades: a sauce that goes well with spaghetti and is also delicious with rice.

SAUCE
2 pounds squid, fresh or frozen

1 large garlic clove
1 red pepper pod, seeded
¼ cup olive oil
½ cup dry white wine
2 cups peeled plum tomatoes
1 teaspoon salt, or to taste
freshly ground pepper

PASTA
6 quarts water
6 teaspoons salt
1¼ pounds spaghetti

Clean the squid (pages 151–153) and cut the tentacles into halves, the body into rings.

Sauté the garlic and pepper pod in the olive oil in a large frying pan over medium heat until the garlic is golden and the pepper pod a deep brown, and then discard both clove and pod. Turn off the heat and let the pan cool a moment.

Add the squid, raise the heat, and sauté for 2 or 3 minutes, or until the squid becomes a delicate pink and the tentacles open up. Add the white wine. Pass the tomatoes through a food mill or coarse sieve and add them to the squid when the wine has almost evaporated. Add the salt and pepper. When the pan comes back to a boil, lower the heat and simmer for about 15 to 20 minutes, or until the squid is tender and the sauce has condensed and darkened in color. Taste for salt and add some if necessary.

Cook and drain the pasta (pages 56–58), put it onto a warm serving platter, dress with the squid sauce, toss gently, and serve immediately. No cheese, please. For 6.

SPAGHETTI AL SUGO DI SEPPIE II /
SPAGHETTI WITH SQUID SAUCE II

SAUCE
2 pounds squid, fresh or frozen
2 garlic cloves
⅓ cup olive oil
1 large onion
3 tablespoons tomato paste, diluted in ½ cup warm water
4 fresh basil leaves
1 teaspoon salt
½ teaspoon sugar

PASTA
6 quarts water
6 teaspoons salt
1¼ pounds spaghetti

Clean the squid (pages 151–153) and cut the tentacles in half, the body into rings.

Sauté the garlic in the olive oil in a large frying pan over medium heat until golden and then discard the cloves. Slice the onion into very thin slices and sauté until limp in the flavored oil. Turn off the heat and let the pan cool a moment.

Add the diluted tomato paste to the onions along with the basil, salt, and sugar. Stirring gently, bring the pan back to a boil and add the squid. Bring back to a boil, lower the heat, and simmer about 15 to 20 minutes, or until the squid is tender. If the sauce becomes too condensed during the cooking, add a bit of hot water.

Cook and drain the pasta (pages 56–58), put it onto a warm serving platter, dress with the squid sauce, toss gently, and serve immediately. For 6.

SPAGHETTI CON LE SARDE ALLA CALABRESE /
SPAGHETTI WITH FRESH SARDINES,
CALABRIAN STYLE

SAUCE
2 pounds large sardines, fresh or frozen
6 tablespoons olive oil
½ cup coarse unseasoned bread crumbs
1½ garlic cloves
½ cup raisins, dark or light

PASTA
6 quarts water
6 teaspoons salt
1¼ pounds spaghetti

Prepare the sardines as for the Sicilian version of this dish (page 82).

Toast the bread crumbs in 1½ tablespoons of the olive oil in a small frying pan until they are golden brown.

Put the remaining olive oil into a large frying pan. Add the garlic and sauté it until golden, and then discard it. Finish cooking the sardines by frying them in the garlic-flavored olive oil along with the raisins. At the last minute add 2 tablespoons of the bread crumbs.

Cook and drain the pasta (pages 56–58), and put it on a warm deep platter. Add the sardines, oil, and raisins. Sprinkle with the last of the bread crumbs, toss gently, and serve. For 6.

VERMICELLI AGLIO, OLIO, E ALICI /
VERMICELLI WITH ANCHOVIES, GARLIC,
AND OLIVE OIL

SAUCE
2 garlic cloves

1 red pepper pod, seeded
¾ cup olive oil
4 salted anchovies, or 8 canned fillets
1 cup unseasoned bread crumbs
½ cup chopped fresh parsley

PASTA
6 quarts water
6 teaspoons salt
1¼ pounds *vermicelli*

Sauté the garlic and red pepper pod in the olive oil (reserving 1 tablespoon) in a medium-sized frying pan over medium heat until the garlic is golden and the red pepper pod dark brown. Then discard both clove and pod.

If using salted anchovies, fillet them (page 15). Add them to the seasoned olive oil, mashing them with a fork, and sauté for 3 minutes. If using canned fillets, drain and mince them. Add them to the seasoned olive oil and sauté until they have disintegrated.

Toast the bread crumbs in the reserved tablespoon of olive oil in a large frying pan over medium heat, until they are well browned. Stir as they cook to prevent burning.

Add the parsley and half the toasted bread crumbs to the anchovies and continue cooking for 5 minutes over very low heat.

Cook and drain the pasta (pages 56–58), and put in a warm, wide, and shallow serving bowl, and dress with the anchovy sauce. Toss well and serve. Serve the remaining toasted bread crumbs as you would grated cheese, to taste. For 6.

VERMICELLI ALLA PUTTANESCA /
VERMICELLI, STREETWALKERS' STYLE

This is a Neapolitan dish served especially in the *trattorie,* small family restaurants, of the port area. The saucy title may show that even if the Neapolitan ladies of the evening have a limited sense of morality, perhaps they make up for it in good eating habits. There are many versions of this sauce, and here are our most favorite three.

Version I

SAUCE

3 salted anchovies, or 6 canned fillets
3 tablespoons capers
24 pitted Sicilian black olives (packed in brine, not dried)
1 garlic clove
¼ cup chopped fresh parsley
freshly ground pepper
½ cup plus 1 tablespoon olive oil
3 tablespoons grated Romano cheese

PASTA

6 quarts water
6 teaspoons salt
1¼ pounds *vermicelli* or thin spaghetti

If using salted anchovies, fillet them (page 15); if using canned, drain them. Mince them with the capers, olives, garlic, and parsley into a paste and put it in the pasta serving bowl. Add the oil, stir well, and add the cheese and a few good grinds of the pepper mill. Stir until perfectly mixed. Put the bowl in a warm place such as on the top of the pasta pot while the water is coming to a boil.

Cook and drain the pasta (pages 56–58), and pour it on top of the sauce in the serving bowl. Mix well and serve. For 6.

Version II

SAUCE

all the ingredients of the first version

1 cup chopped fresh peeled plum tomatoes

Proceed as in the first version. Add the chopped tomatoes to the minced herbs when you add the oil, mix well, and serve as in the first version. For 6.

Version III

SAUCE
1 garlic clove
½ cup olive oil
3 salted anchovies, or 6 canned fillets
24 pitted Sicilian black olives (packed in brine, not dried)
4 tablespoons chopped fresh parsley
1 cup chopped fresh peeled plum tomatoes
freshly ground pepper
3 tablespoons grated Romano cheese

Sauté the garlic in the olive oil until golden and then discard the clove. If using salted anchovies, fillet them (page 15); if using canned, drain them.

While the pasta water is coming to a boil, finely chop together the anchovies, capers, olives, and parsley and add to the flavored olive oil. Add the chopped tomatoes and pepper and bring to a gentle boil. Cook only as long as it takes to cook the pasta, or about 8 to 10 minutes.

Drain the cooked pasta, put it into a warm serving bowl, dress with the sauce, and sprinkle on the cheese. Toss and serve immediately. For 6.

VERMICELLI ALLE COZZE /
VERMICELLI WITH MUSSEL SAUCE

SAUCE
3 pounds mussels

2 garlic cloves
1 red pepper pod, seeded
⅓ cup olive oil
3 tablespoons tomato paste, or 2 cups peeled plum tomatoes
salt to taste
2 tablespoons chopped fresh parsley

PASTA
6 quarts water
6 teaspoons salt
1¼ pounds *vermicelli* or thin spaghetti

Clean the mussels (page 151).

Put just enough water in a big pot to cover the bottom, bring to a boil, add the mussels, cover, and steam for about 5 minutes or until the shells are open. Set aside to cool.

When cool enough to handle, remove the mussels from their shells, saving their juice. Strain the juice through a cheesecloth-lined sieve and reserve it. Cut the biggest mussels into halves.

Sauté the garlic and the pepper pod in the olive oil over medium high heat, until the garlic is golden and the pepper pod a deep brown. Then discard the clove and pod and let the oil cool.

If using tomato paste, dilute it with 1 cup of the mussel juice and add it to the flavored olive oil. Simmer about 10 minutes, add the mussels, and simmer another 5 minutes. Taste for salt and add some if necessary.

If using plum tomatoes, cut them open, remove the seeds, and cut the tomatoes into small pieces. Add with the strained mussel juice to the olive oil and simmer until sauce consistency is reached. Add the mussels and simmer another 5 minutes.

Cook and drain the pasta (pages 56–58), and put it into a warm serving bowl or onto a warm platter. Dress with the mussel sauce, sprinkle with parsley, mix well and serve. For 6.

VERMICELLI ALLE COZZE IN BIANCO /
VERMICELLI WITH WHITE MUSSEL SAUCE

SAUCE
3 pounds mussels
⅔ cup olive oil
2 garlic cloves
1 red pepper pod, seeded
salt to taste
2 tablespoons chopped fresh parsley

PASTA
6 quarts water
6 teaspoons salt
1¼ pounds *vermicelli* or thin spaghetti

Clean the mussels (page 151).

Put just enough water in a big pot to cover the bottom, bring to a boil, add the mussels, cover, and steam for about 5 minutes, or until the shells are open. Set aside to cool.

Sauté the garlic and the pepper pod in the olive oil over a brisk heat, until the garlic is golden and the pepper a deep brown. Then discard clove and pod and let the oil cool.

Remove the mussels from their shells, saving their juice, and cut the biggest ones into halves. Add the mussels to the flavored olive oil. Strain the mussel juice through a cheesecloth-lined sieve and add 1 cup of it to the olive oil. Simmer until the oil and the juice are blended together and have condensed a bit. Taste for salt and add some if necessary.

Cook and drain the pasta (pages 56–58), and put it into a warm serving dish, either a deep serving platter or a wide, shallow bowl. Dress with the mussels and their sauce. Sprinkle with the parsley, mix well, and serve. The mussels sink to the bottom and so must be distributed equitably after the pasta is served. For 6.

VERMICELLI CON ALICI E POMODORI /
VERMICELLI WITH ANCHOVIES AND TOMATOES

SAUCE
1 garlic clove
1 large onion
4 tablespoons olive oil
2 cups peeled plum tomatoes
12 fresh basil leaves
freshly ground pepper
4 to 5 salted anchovies, or 8 to 10 small canned fillets
salt to taste
½ cup coarsely chopped fresh parsley
grated Romano cheese to taste

PASTA
6 quarts water
6 teaspoons salt
1½ pounds *vermicelli* or thin spaghetti

Finely chop the garlic or mash it with the flat side of a big knife. Cut the onion into very thin slices and sauté with the garlic in the olive oil in a large frying pan over medium heat until golden and limp. If you didn't chop the garlic, remove the mashed clove from the pan when golden.

Cut the tomatoes into chunks, and add them to the onions.

Tear half the basil leaves into bits, and add them to the simmering tomatoes and onions. Add a bit of freshly ground pepper and cook for about 15 minutes.

If using salted anchovies, fillet them (page 15); if using canned, drain them. Mash the anchovies with a fork, and add to the simmering tomatoes and onions.

When the sauce has darkened and condensed (in about 10 minutes or so), taste for salt and add some if the anchovies haven't given enough flavor to the sauce.

While you are bringing the pasta water to a boil, chop the remaining basil leaves and add them to the parsley. Cook and drain the pasta (pages 56–58), put it on a warm serving platter, and dress with the sauce. Toss gently and add the chopped basil and parsley. Sprinkle with the cheese, toss again, and serve immediately. For 6.

ZITI AL POMODORO E TONNO /
MACARONI WITH TOMATO-AND-TUNA SAUCE

SAUCE
1 garlic clove
3 salted anchovies, or 6 canned fillets
1 onion
4 tablespoons olive oil
1½ cups peeled plum tomatoes
1 7-ounce can Italian tuna
½ teaspoon oregano
freshly ground pepper
salt to taste
4 tablespoons grated Romano cheese

PASTA
6 quarts water
6 teaspoons salt
1¼ pounds macaroni (*ziti*)

Put the garlic on a cutting board and mash it with the flat side of a big knife.

If using salted anchovies, fillet them (page 15); if using canned anchovies, drain them. Coarsely chop the onion, and then mince it together thoroughly with the garlic and anchovies.

Sauté the garlic-onion-anchovy mixture in the olive oil in a large frying pan over medium heat for 5 minutes, or until the onion bits are translucent and the anchovies have disintegrated.

Cool the pan a minute or two (to avoid spattering) and add

the tomatoes, crushing them with a wooden spoon as they go in. Bring the pan to a boil, cover, lower the heat and cook for 15 minutes. Add the tuna, oregano, and pepper. Stir again to break up the tuna a bit. Taste for salt and add some if necessary. Continue cooking another 5 minutes or so, or until the sauce has condensed a bit and the color darkened.

Cook and drain the pasta (pages 56–58) and add it to the simmering sauce. Add the cheese, raise the heat, mix well, and serve immediately. For 6.

MINESTRE / SOUPS

Minestre covers all kinds and textures of soups from the light fish and vegetable broths to the hearty soup of soups, *minestrone*. Vegetable broth is easy to make and can be made ahead of time for use as stock at a future date. It keeps well for a week or so in a sealed glass jar in the refrigerator.

As for rice in soups, we recommend using long-grain rice. It can take long cooking without losing its shape, which cannot be said of the treated rice that takes a minute to cook.

We use fresh vegetables whenever possible; otherwise we take advantage of the frozen, but never the canned (with the exception of tomatoes). In using the frozen, we suggest only those which come close enough to the fresh to merit inclusion. Paradoxically, sometimes a frozen vegetable is tastier and more economical than a vegetable that has traveled a long way and is fresh in name only. A frozen vegetable can be used to satisfy an off-season whim and make everybody happy.

In this selection of *minestre* recipes, we've tried to stick to those that can be made with ingredients usually available in today's American market.

As for the cheese that's served with soup, it's the Italian custom to set the table with a small dish of grated cheese so that everyone can add a sprinkling as he or she wishes, *a piacére,* to please.

BRODO MAGRO / VEGETABLE BROTH

Here's a nonmeat broth that can be served by itself with a bit of butter and Parmesan cheese, or with a small shaped pasta or rice, or it can be used as stock in the preparation of other soups. The delicately flavored boiled potatoes that are left over can be recycled any way you wish.

6 medium potatoes
3 quarts cold water
3 onions
2 carrots
2 celery stalks with leaves
4 peeled plum tomatoes
3 fresh basil leaves
3 parsley sprigs
1 bay leaf
3 teaspoons salt, or to taste
5 peppercorns

If using new potatoes, scrub clean and cook with their jackets on; if using old potatoes with tough skins, peel them before cooking. Put them in the soup pot with the water. While the pot is coming to a boil, peel and cut the onions in half and scrub the carrots and celery stalks. Add them and the tomatoes to the pot along with the herbs, salt, and peppercorns.

When the pot boils, reduce the heat to simmer, cover, and cook gently for at least 2 hours.

Pour the broth through a fine sieve into a clean pot. Use as needed.

If the cooked potatoes have survived the ordeal whole (some do and some don't), they can be used for a *frittata* (pages 196–197), a salad, making *Cazzilli* (pages 213–214), or for frying. For 6.

Fish broth is a basic recipe with two versions to its name: rich and poor. The rich *brodo di pesce* is made with the kind of fish you would poach and serve as a second course. The poor version is made with heads, tails, and cheeks that are thrown away after they've flavored the broth.

2½ to 3 pounds fish
2 garlic cloves
4 tablespoons olive oil
2 salted anchovies, or 4 canned fillets
3 tablespoons chopped fresh parsley
2 cups (1 pound) fresh peeled plum tomatoes
2 quarts warm water
1 small onion
1 small carrot
1 celery stalk
2½ teaspoons salt
2 bay leaves

If making the rich version, use halibut, haddock, fresh cod, striped sea bass, or any type of meaty fish that lends itself to poaching, but avoid oily types such as mackerel. Have the fish cleaned and scaled, but leave on the heads and tails for added flavor.

If using the poor version, a pound of fish cheeks, a pound of heads and tails, and a pound of any inexpensive (but non-oily) fish will do.

Sauté the garlic in the olive oil in a big, heavy soup pot until golden and then discard.

If using salted anchovies, fillet them (page 15); if using canned, drain them. Chop them with the parsley, and sauté in the flavored oil, stirring gently until the anchovies have disintegrated.

Cut the tomatoes into chunks and add to the pot. Cook uncovered over medium heat about 10 to 15 minutes, or until the tomatoes have cooked and a semi-sauce has developed. Put the fish on top of the tomatoes, add the salt, and when the pot starts to boil, lower the heat and cover well. If the cover doesn't fit perfectly, slip a round of brown paper between pot and cover to seal. Cook over low heat for 15 minutes, or until the fish flakes easily.

If using the fish for a second course, remove it at this time. If using bones and bits, leave them in.

Add the warm water. Peel and slice the onion and carrot; cut up the celery, and add all three with the bay leaves to the pot. Bring to a boil, and boil gently for 15 minutes.

Taste for salt and adjust seasoning if necessary.

Put the broth through a sieve and use as a *minestra* with *capellini* (page 102), or bone the poached fish and serve with the fish broth. For 6.

CIPOLLATA / UMBRIAN ONION SOUP

2 pounds onions
5 tablespoons olive oil
2 teaspoons salt
freshly ground pepper
5 fresh basil leaves
2 cups peeled plum tomatoes
1 quart water
4 tablespoons grated Parmesan cheese
2 eggs
6 slices Italian bread (optional), toasted or fried in olive oil

Slice the onions into the thinnest possible slivers. Soak them overnight in abundant water in a pot with a tight-fitting lid.

Drain the onions thoroughly, shaking out as much water as possible. Sauté them in olive oil in a soup pot, adding the salt and pepper. Tear up the basil leaves and add them to the onions. Cover the pot and continue cooking for about 10 minutes, or until the onions have wilted and the liquid has been almost totally absorbed.

Put the tomatoes through a food mill and add them to the onions. Pour in the water, mix well, cover, and cook over medium heat for 1½ hours.

Remove from the heat and sprinkle in the Parmesan cheese, 1 tablespoon at a time. Let cool a bit. Beat the eggs, and mix them into the soup, stirring rapidly all the time.

Serve hot (on the toasted Italian bread if you wish a totally hearty soup). For 6 to 8.

CREMA DI FUNGHI /
CREAM OF MUSHROOM SOUP

1 pound mushrooms, preferably golden
4 tablespoons unsalted butter
1 garlic clove
1 cup chopped fresh parsley
2 teaspoons salt
freshly ground white pepper
½ teaspoon freshly grated nutmeg
½ cup Marsala wine
1 recipe *Besciamella* (page 20)
1½ to 2 cups Vegetable Broth (page 97)

Clean and slice the mushrooms, and put them into a 3-quart soup pot with the butter. Sauté for 5 minutes.

Chop the garlic and add to the soup pot with the parsley, salt, pepper (2 or 3 twists of the mill), nutmeg, and Marsala. Cook another 5 minutes. Remove from the heat.

Make the *besciamella* and add it to the mushrooms in the soup pot.

Add 1½ cups of the vegetable broth to the mushrooms. Stir and heat over medium heat until hot but not boiling. Taste for salt, add some if necessary, and if you prefer a less thick soup, add a bit more broth. For 6.

MALFATTINI CON VERDURE /
VEGETABLE SOUP WITH PASTA BITS

Malfattini comes from the word *malfatto,* poorly done, which in this case refers to pasta cut haphazardly into odd, small shapes about as big as a grain of rice. If making homemade pasta, add a pinch of nutmeg to the ingredients for *pasta all'uovo.* If using commercially made egg noodles, smash them up to look like the real thing.

PASTA

1 2-egg batch *Pasta all'uovo* (pages 47–55)
¼ teaspoon freshly grated nutmeg
    OR
½ pound wide egg noodles

SOUP

4 tablespoons olive oil
4 tablespoons unsalted butter
1 celery stalk
1 large carrot
1 small onion
1 pound fresh greens (a mixture of spinach, lettuce, romaine,
    endive, and escarole, OR spinach alone)
1 tablespoon tomato paste
2½ quarts water
3½ teaspoons salt
4 to 6 tablespoons grated Parmesan cheese, minimum

If using homemade pasta, mix as in the recipe, adding the freshly grated nutmeg, and after it is kneaded and smooth, roll it out to a sheet ⅛-inch thick, using either the long rolling pin or the pasta machine. Cut into 3″ x 5″ rectangles, flour lightly on both sides, and let dry for ½ hour on kitchen towels or cookie sheets. Once dry enough so that the pasta pieces don't stick to each other, make a deck of 4 or 5 rectangles and chop them haphazardly with a very sharp knife. The resulting *malfattini* should be about the size of big grains of rice. Once all the pasta is cut, spread out on cloths to dry completely. Depending on room temperature and humidity, 1 to 2 hours should do, but *malfattini* can dry longer. Save any small crumbs resulting from the cuttings. They should end up in the soup too and make it even thicker.

If using commercial egg noodles, fold them up in a clean kitchen towel, and then roll over and over them with a rolling pin until they are smashed to bits.

Melt the butter with the olive oil in the bottom of a big soup pot. Chop the celery, carrot, and onion well, and sauté them in the butter and oil for 15 minutes over medium heat, or until golden and limp.

Wash the greens thoroughly, and in a big pot with a good cover steam them in the water that clings to the leaves. Stir a couple of times as the greens steam. When tender, drain them thoroughly, cool slightly, and chop well.

Add the chopped greens, the tomato paste, water, and salt to the soup pot. Bring to a boil, lower the heat, and cook covered for 15 minutes.

Bring the soup to a good boil, add the pasta (including the crumbs), stirring as it goes in. Continue cooking until the pasta is tender, about 5 minutes, stirring occasionally.

Serve with the Parmesan cheese. For 6.

MINESTRA IN BRODO DI PESCE /
PASTA IN FISH BROTH

1 receipe Fish Broth, poor man's version (pages 98–99)
½ pound *capellini*

Make the fish broth using bones, heads, tails, cheeks. After you have strained the cooked broth, bring it to a boil, add the *capellini*, breaking them in half as they go into the pot. Bring back to a boil and cook for about 5 minutes, or until the pasta is *al dente*. Serve in soup bowls immediately. For 6.

MINESTRA DI CECI / CHICK-PEA SOUP

1 tablespoon dried rosemary or 1 fresh sprig
2 garlic cloves
½ cup olive oil
1 tablespoon tomato paste, diluted in ½ cup warm water
1 1-pound can chick-peas
8 cups warm water
2 teaspoons salt, or to taste
½ pound small macaroni shapes (*tubetti,* shells, *cannolicchi*)
freshly ground pepper

Sauté the rosemary and garlic in the olive oil until the garlic is golden. Remove the garlic. Add the diluted tomato paste to the flavored oil. Stir and cook for 3 minutes.

Mash up 2 or 3 tablespoons of the chick-peas to a paste and add to the tomato and oil along with the remaining chick-peas and the liquid they are canned in. Add the remaining water and the salt and bring to a boil.

Add the pasta, bring back to a boil, stirring from time to time, and cook until the pasta is *al dente.*

Check for salt and add some if necessary. Serve hot or warm with lots of freshly ground pepper. For 6.

MINESTRA DI ERBE PASSATE / VEGETABLE SOUP

For a really rich soup, use vegetable broth as your base, but if none is handy, plain water will do nicely.

1 small onion
5 parsley sprigs
1 celery stalk with leaves
1 small carrot
4 fresh basil leaves
5 tablespoons olive oil
1 10-ounce package frozen spinach, thawed, or 1 pound fresh
1 head romaine lettuce

½ head escarole
1 cup peeled plum tomatoes, chopped
1 potato, peeled and diced
2 teaspoons salt
freshly ground pepper
7 cups hot Vegetable Broth (page 97) or water

Chop together the onion, parsley, celery, carrot, and basil until they form a paste. Sauté in the olive oil in a big soup pot over medium heat for about 10 minutes, or until golden.

Wash the romaine and escarole (and spinach, if using fresh) thoroughly and cut up coarsely.

Add all the greens, including the spinach, to the flavored olive oil, add salt, and stir until they begin to wilt. Add the tomatoes, potatoes, and pepper (4 or 5 twists of the mill). Stir well, cover, and cook for 10 minutes, stirring frequently. Add the hot broth or water, bring to a boil, lower the heat, and simmer 30 minutes, or until the vegetables are really well cooked.

Let the soup cool a bit, and then either pass it through a vegetable mill or blend it, 2 to 3 cups at a time. Bring to a boil (in a clean pot), taste for seasonings and adjust as desired. Serve hot. For 6.

MINESTRA DI FUNGHI / MUSHROOM SOUP

This clear mushroom soup made with the thinnest of pasta, *capelli d'angelo* or angel's hair, is one *minestra* you have to eat with a fork as well as a spoon.

¾ to 1 pound big, fresh mushrooms
7 cups water
2½ teaspoons salt
¼ cup olive oil
4 to 6 tablespoons grated Parmesan cheese (minimum)
½ pound *capelli d'angelo* or the finest *vermicelli*

Clean and slice the mushrooms and put them in a big soup pot with 7 cups of water. Add the salt and bring to a boil. Reduce the heat and cook 10 minutes, or until the mushrooms are tender.

Raise the heat and add the olive oil. Sprinkle in 2 tablespoons of cheese, stir, and let boil for 3 to 4 minutes. Break the *capelli d'angelo* in half and add them to the boiling pot. Cook until the pasta is *al dente* (about 4 minutes). Serve in soup plates with the last of the cheese to be sprinkled on individually, according to taste. For 6.

MINESTRA DI MAGRO CON CAVOLO /
LEAN CABBAGE SOUP

1 small cabbage
¼ cup olive oil
½ cup chopped fresh parsley
1 celery stalk with leaves
1 onion
8 cups Fish Broth (pages 98–99)
½ cup long-grain rice
salt to taste
freshly ground pepper

Tear off the outside, heavy leaves of the cabbage and discard them along with the core. Cut the rest of the cabbage into thin strips and wash in cold water. Drain thoroughly.

Put the olive oil into a soup pot. Finely chop together the parsley, celery, and onion, add to the olive oil, and sauté over medium heat 10 minutes, or until golden-green and limp. Add the cabbage and cook about 5 minutes, stirring constantly, until the cabbage is wilted.

Bring the fish broth to a boil, add it to the cabbage, cover, and cook over low heat for ½ hour.

Add the rice and cook 15 minutes more, or until the rice is *al dente*. Check the liquid in the soup during this time, because if the lid isn't on tight, too much steam escapes from the pot so that the soup becomes too dry and the rice doesn't cook properly. If this should happen, add a bit of hot water, and the next time you use that pot, slip brown paper between cover and pot to make a good seal.

Taste for salt and add some if desired. Add freshly ground pepper to taste. Serve hot. For 6.

MINESTRA DI MAGRO CON FAGIOLI /
MEATLESS BEAN SOUP

3 garlic cloves
5 tablespoons olive oil
10 fresh peeled plum tomatoes, cut in chunks
10 big fresh mushrooms, sliced
1 pound canned *cannellini* (white beans)
1½ cups long-grain rice
3 teaspoons salt
4 cups warm water
3 heaping tablespoons chopped fresh parsley
freshly ground pepper
3 to 4 tablespoons grated Parmesan cheese

Sauté the garlic in the olive oil in a big soup pot until golden brown and then discard the cloves. Let the oil cool a moment. Then add the tomatoes and mushrooms. Cook for 5 minutes.

Add the canned beans, liquid and all. Add the rice, salt, and warm water. Bring to a boil, cover, reduce the heat, and cook 15 minutes, or until the rice is tender. Stir once or twice while cooking.

Uncover the pot, stir in the parsley, and add the pepper. Serve the soup hot with a sprinkling of Parmesan cheese. For 6.

MINESTRONE COL PESTO /
MINESTRONE WITH PESTO

This is a truly big soup, filled with summer vegetables and accented with *pesto*, that delicious basil sauce which can be made ahead of time and used sparingly in so many dishes.

1 cup fresh shell or kidney beans
2½ quarts water
3½ teaspoons salt
2 potatoes
2 carrots
2 leeks
2 tomatoes
1 onion
2 zucchini
1 celery stalk with leaves
1 handful of escarole
4 tablespoons olive oil
2 cups small macaroni (*tubetti*, shells, *cavatelli*)
2 tablespoons *Pesto* (pages 21–22)
2 tablespoons grated Parmesan cheese, minimum
2 tablespoons grated Romano cheese, minimum

Shell the beans. Bring the water to a boil, add the salt and beans, and bring back to a boil.

Peel the potatoes, carrots, the outer part of the leeks, the tomatoes, and onion. Cut them into small pieces. Wash the zucchini, celery, and escarole, and cut them up also.

Add the prepared vegetables and the olive oil to the boiling bean pot. When it comes back to a boil, cover, lower the heat, and simmer gently for 2 hours. The soup should now be thick and all the vegetables really cooked.

Add the pasta, cook another 15 minutes, or until the pasta is *al dente*. Add the *pesto* and stir well.

Serve with the two grated cheeses, letting everyone choose which one and how much he or she wants. For 8.

Pancotto, cooked bread, is really a clear, light tomato soup, each bowl of which holds a toasted slice of bread with a poached egg on top. Almost every region of Italy has its own *pancotto.* This one is the most suitable for the Italian bread available in this country.

  1 pound fresh ripe plum tomatoes
  1 garlic clove
  1 celery stalk with leaves
  1 bay leaf
  3 tablespoons chopped fresh parsley
  4 tablespoons olive oil
  2 teaspoons salt
  freshly ground pepper
  8 cups hot water
  6 slices day-old Italian bread, toasted
  6 eggs
  3 tablespoons grated Parmesan cheese (optional)

Peel the tomatoes and chop them coarsely. Chop together the garlic, celery, and bay leaf, and put them along with the parsley and olive oil into a soup pot over high heat. Stir, and then add the salt, pepper, and water. Bring to a boil, lower the heat, cover the pot, and boil gently for ½ hour.

Uncover the pot, taste for salt and add some if necessary, and boil another 15 minutes.

Toast the bread well on both sides and put 1 slice in each of 6 soup plates.

When the soup is done, strain it through a sieve or send it through a food mill into a soup tureen or other pot. Cover and keep hot.

Put enough of the tomato soup to poach the eggs into a frying pan, bring to a gentle boil, and poach the eggs in it. As soon as the eggs are cooked, remove them with a slotted spoon or spatula and put one on top of each piece of toast in the bowls. Ladle the rest of the soup over the eggs. Sprinkle with cheese, if you wish, and serve hot. For 6.

PASTA E FASOI / BEAN SOUP WITH PASTA

2 garlic cloves
4 tablespoons olive oil
3 tablespoons chopped fresh parsley
1 fresh rosemary sprig or 1 tablespoon dried
2 heaping tablespoons tomato paste, diluted in 1 cup warm
water
1 1-pound can kidney or shell beans
7 cups warm water
2 teaspoons salt
½ pound small shaped macaroni (elbows, shells)
4 to 6 tablespoons grated Parmesan cheese, minimum

Sauté the garlic in the oil in a big soup pot until golden and then discard the cloves. Add the parsley to the oil along with the rosemary. Continue cooking for about 2 minutes over medium heat so that the herbs flavor the oil.

Add the diluted tomato paste to the flavored oil. Cook for another two minutes. Add the beans with the liquid they are canned in, and the warm water. Add the salt, bring to a boil, add the pasta, bring back to a boil, and cook until the pasta is *al dente*. Stir while the pasta is cooking.

When the pasta is done, remove the pot from the heat and stir in 3 tablespoons of the cheese. Serve hot with the remaining cheese, which may be added according to individual taste. For 6.

RISO ALLA FRIULANA / RICE WITH LEMON SAUCE

This thick soup can be described as a special phenomenon halfway between *minestre* and *risotti,* a compromise that's a pleasure to make.

2 quarts water
2 tablespoons unsalted butter
2 teaspoons salt
2 cups long-grain rice
4 large egg yolks
juice of 1½ lemons
9 tablespoons grated Parmesan cheese, minimum
2 tablespoons coarsely chopped fresh parsley

Combine the water, butter, salt, and rice in a big pot over high heat. Bring to a boil, stir, cover, lower the heat, and cook for about 13 minutes, or until the rice is *al dente*. Stir occasionally.

Put the egg yolks in a soup tureen, beat them well, and add the lemon juice slowly, beating as you pour. Beat in 3 tablespoons of the cheese.

When the rice is cooked, pour it slowly, liquid and all, onto the eggs, stirring as you pour so that the eggs coat the rice and are not cooked in lumps by it. Finally stir in 3 more tablespoons of cheese.

Sprinkle with the chopped parsley, and serve with the remaining cheese to be added as you please. For 6.

RISO MARIÀ / RICE WITH SPINACH AND EGGS

The word *marià*, in dialect, means married. In this case the rice cooked with spinach is married to eggs mixed with cheese. "Rice" in Italian is always singular and masculine, and "eggs" are feminine but only when plural: hence the vague possibility of a wedding. Confusing, perhaps, but proper. The result is a mellow, creamy soup whose ceremony is very simple, short, and delightful.

2 10-ounce packages frozen chopped spinach, or 1½ pounds
   fresh
3 teaspoons salt
5 tablespoons unsalted butter

1½ cups long-grain rice
2 eggs
7 tablespoons grated Parmesan cheese

If you use frozen spinach, defrost and cook in at least 2 quarts of boiling salted water. Drain, reserving the spinach water, squeeze dry, and mince well. If you use fresh spinach, wash thoroughly, discard the thickest of the stems, and cook in at least 2 quarts of boiling salted water. Drain, reserving the spinach water, squeeze dry, and mince well.

Melt the butter in a big soup pot, add the minced spinach, and sauté for 5 minutes. Add 1½ quarts of spinach water, bring it to a boil, and add the rice and salt. Cover the pot and cook for about 13 minutes, or until the rice is *al dente*. Stir occasionally while cooking, and if the rice absorbs so much water that it's dry, add a bit more spinach water or plain hot water.

Beat the eggs well, add the Parmesan cheese, and beat some more.

When the rice is perfectly cooked, remove it from the heat and cool it 5 minutes or so.

Stir in the beaten eggs and mix well, so that the eggs not only lend their color throughout but the heat of the warm rice cooks them.

Either serve right away, or let stand for a few minutes, during which time the "wedded rice" will become even thicker. For 6.

STRACCIATA CON ZUCCHINE /
ZUCCHINI SOUP WITH BEATEN EGGS

This is a vegetable version of *stracciatella,* the broth with beaten eggs which seem to be torn to bits (*stracciate*) by the boiling.

6 small to medium-sized zucchini
3 tablespoons olive oil
3 tablespoons unsalted butter
2 quarts warm water

2½ teaspoons salt
freshly ground pepper
6 tablespoons chopped fresh parsley
3 fresh basil leaves
3 eggs
3 tablespoons grated Romano cheese

Wash the zucchini, cut off the ends, and slice into quarters lengthwise. Slice the quarters into ½-inch pieces.

Put the oil and butter in a big soup pot over medium heat. When the butter has melted, add the zucchini and sauté for 5 minutes, stirring gently. Add 2 quarts of warm water, the salt, and pepper (a few twists of the mill). Bring to a boil, lower the heat, and boil gently for 10 minutes.

Finely chop together the parsley and basil. Beat the eggs, add the herbs and the cheese, and mix well.

When the zucchini are cooked, pour the egg mixture into the bubbling soup, stir with a wire whisk, and turn off the heat when the bits of egg are cooked and floating throughout the soup. Serve immediately. For 6.

ZUPPA CONTADINA / PEASANT SOUP

1 small onion
1 celery stalk
1 carrot
1 garlic clove
3 cups chopped fresh parsley, including stems
½ cup olive oil
1 pound fresh shell beans
5 cups hot water
2 teaspoons salt
freshly ground pepper
1 pound fresh Swiss chard
6 slices day-old Italian bread (optional), toasted or fried in
   olive oil

Chop together very finely the herb and vegetable seasonings (the first 5 ingredients). Sauté in the olive oil over medium heat in a big soup pot for 5 minutes, or until the colors start to change and the bits of herbs are limp.

Shell the beans and add them to the flavored olive oil. Add the water, salt, and pepper. Bring to a boil, lower the heat, and cook 20 minutes, or until the beans are almost tender.

Wash the chard thoroughly (at least 3 times), trim the stalks of coarse ribs, and chop into ½- to 1-inch bits.

When the beans are practically cooked, add the chard, raise the heat, and continue cooking another 10 minutes or until the bits of chard stems are tender to the bite. Taste for salt and add some if desired.

If including Italian bread with this soup, put 1 slice of toast in each soup plate, and ladle the hot soup over it. For 6.

ZUPPA DI ASPARAGI / ASPARAGUS SOUP

This dish, also called *stracciata di asparagi,* is another one of many recipes in which beaten eggs and cheese are added to a soup and cooked into *stracci,* or rags. But don't let the translation mislead you: to the palate, these rags are high fashion.

2 pounds fresh asparagus, or 2 10-ounce packages frozen cut
1 garlic clove
⅓ cup olive oil
freshly ground pepper
7 cups hot water
1½ teaspoons salt
4 medium eggs or 3 extra-large
6 tablespoons grated Parmesan cheese
6 slices Italian bread (optional), toasted or fried

If using fresh asparagus, break off and discard the root ends, wash the stalks thoroughly, and cut into bite-sized pieces; if using frozen asparagus, thaw at room temperature.

Finely chop the garlic or put it through a garlic press. Sauté the asparagus and garlic in the olive oil in a big soup pot over medium heat for 8 minutes, or until the asparagus is really tender. Season with pepper (4 to 6 twists of the mill) as the asparagus cooks.

Add the hot water and salt, and bring to a boil. Continue boiling for about 5 minutes to flavor the water.

Beat the eggs with the grated cheese. Add the beaten eggs to the boiling soup, stirring with a wire whisk until the soup comes back to a boil and the eggs are cooked.

Serve hot, either ladled over toasted bread or not, in soup plates. For 6.

ZUPPA DI BROCCOLI / BROCCOLI SOUP

1½ pounds broccoli
4 tablespoons olive oil
1 garlic clove
1 red pepper pod, seeded
2 tablespoons tomato paste, diluted in 1 cup hot water
7 cups hot water
3 teaspoons salt
freshly ground pepper
½ pound *spaghettini* or *linguine*
grated Parmesan cheese

Wash the broccoli, cut off all the flowerets, and cut them into little bits. Discard the thick center stems.

Put the olive oil into a large soup pot over medium heat. Add the garlic and pepper pod, sauté until the garlic is golden and the red pepper a deep brown, and then remove them.

Let the pot cool a minute. Add the diluted tomato paste to the flavored olive oil. Bring to a boil, add the broccoli bits, 1½ teaspoons of the salt, and pepper. Stir and cook about 8 minutes, or until the broccoli is tender.

Add the remaining hot water and the rest of the salt, and bring the pot to a boil. Add the pasta, breaking it into 1- to 2-inch lengths as it goes into the pot. Cook 6 minutes, stirring from time to time, or until the pasta is *al dente.*

Serve hot with the grated Parmesan cheese, as desired. For 6.

ZUPPA DI CECI E FAGIOLI /
CHICK-PEA–AND–BEAN SOUP

Traditionally this soup used dried chick-peas, dried kidney beans, and dried mushrooms, but today's canned peas and beans do a very good job. As for the dried mushrooms, Italian ones are increasingly expensive and hard to find, and the Chinese dried mushrooms do not have the right flavor. So we've substituted fresh mushrooms in such quantity as to approximate the original flavor. We even think that the texture they add is a great improvement over the original.

8 big fresh mushrooms, or 2 ounces dried Italian mushrooms
1 garlic clove
1 medium onion
1 carrot
1 celery stalk
4 tablespoons olive oil
1 cup peeled plum tomatoes, crushed
1 pound Swiss chard
2 teaspoons salt
1 1-pound can chick-peas with canning liquid
1 cup (½ 1-pound can) canned kidney beans with all the canning liquid
3 cups hot water
freshly ground pepper (optional)

If you are using dried mushrooms, soak them in a cup of warm water for 15 to 20 minutes, squeeze them dry, and slice into bite-sized pieces.

Chop together very finely the garlic, onion, carrot, and celery.

Sauté in the olive oil in a soup pot over medium heat 4 to 5 minutes, or until limp. Add the plum tomatoes and bring back to a boil.

Wash the chard thoroughly, discard the heaviest stems, chop the rest coarsely into pieces no bigger than bite-sized. Add to the bubbling tomatoes. Add the salt, stir, and cook until the chard is limp.

Add the canning liquids and bring to a boil.

If using fresh mushrooms, slice them and add to the boiling soup. When the soup boils again, add the chick-peas and beans. When the pot comes back to a boil, add the hot water.

If using dried mushrooms, add them now.

Cover the pot, bring to a boil, lower the heat, and boil gently for 15 minutes. Taste for salt and add some if you wish. You may also add some freshly ground pepper, as desired. For 6.

ZUPPA DI CIPOLLA / ONION SOUP

Onion soup, staple of the European working class, has always had an important place on Italian tables. In this Calabrian version the onions are flavored with red pepper and Romano cheese.

    2 pounds small onions
    4 tablespoons olive oil
    2 tablespoons unsalted butter
    1 red pepper pod, seeded
    3 teaspoons salt
    2 quarts hot water
    6 tablespoons grated Romano cheese
    6 thick slices Italian bread, toasted

Peel and slice the onions into very thin slices. Put them in a soup pot with the olive oil, butter, pepper pod, and salt. Sauté over medium heat, stirring almost constantly, until limp and pale gold. Remove and discard the pepper pod.

Add the hot water, bring to a boil, cover, lower the heat, and boil gently for 45 minutes. Then uncover, taste for salt, add some if necessary, and cook another 15 minutes uncovered.

Sprinkle in the cheese, 1 tablespoon at a time, stirring constantly. Ladle onto the toasted bread in soup plates and serve hot. For 6 to 8.

ZUPPA DI FAGIOLI / WHITE BEAN SOUP

1 pound cabbage
1 celery stalk
1 medium onion
5 fresh plum tomatoes, peeled and chopped
1 5-inch fresh rosemary sprig or 1 teaspoon dried
½ cup olive oil
1 1-pound can *cannellini* (white beans) with canning liquid
5 cups water
1½ teaspoons salt, or to taste
freshly ground pepper
6 slices Italian bread (optional), toasted or fried in olive oil
grated Parmesan cheese (optional)

Core the cabbage, discard the toughest outer leaves, and chop it coarsely, along with the celery and onion, into bite-sized pieces.

Sauté the chopped vegetables (including the tomatoes) and the rosemary in the olive oil in a soup pot over medium heat until they begin to wilt, stirring as they cook.

Add the liquid from the *cannellini* can, the water, salt, and pepper. Bring to a boil, lower the heat, and boil gently for 15 minutes, or until the celery and cabbage are tender. Then add the *cannellini* and gently boil another 10 minutes.

Serve the soup hot. If using the Italian bread, put a slice in each bowl and pour the soup over it. If using the Parmesan cheese, sprinkle as desired over each serving. For 6.

ZUPPA DI LENTICCHIE / LENTIL SOUP

    1½ cups dried lentils
    3 garlic cloves
    4 tablespoons olive oil
    1 medium onion
    4 celery stalks with leaves
    6 parsley sprigs
    3 tablespoons tomato paste, diluted in ½ cup warm water
    2 quarts warm water
    2½ teaspoons salt

Check the lentils a handful at a time for bits of chaff or stone. Wash briefly in a colander under cold water.

Sauté the garlic in the olive oil in a soup pot until golden and then discard the cloves.

Chop together the onion, celery leaves, and parsley, and sauté in the flavored olive oil about 10 minutes, or until golden-green and wilted.

Add the diluted tomato paste to the minced vegetable and herbs and cook for 10 minutes.

Add the clean lentils, the water, and the salt. Bring to a boil, lower the heat, and boil gently for 15 minutes.

Chop the celery stalks into ½-inch pieces and add to the lentils. Continue slow boiling for 15 minutes, or until the lentils and celery are thoroughly cooked.

Taste for salt and add some if necessary. Serve hot. For 6 to 8.

ZUPPA DI PESCE D'ORTONA /
FISH SOUP FROM ORTONA

    4 tablespoons olive oil
    1 dried red pepper pod, seeded
    2 cups peeled plum tomatoes, cut in chunks
    1 sweet pepper, roasted and cut in strips (page 36)

¼ teaspoon oregano
½ teaspoon salt, or to taste
freshly ground pepper
1 pound squid, cleaned and cut in rings (pages 151–153)
¾ cup dry white wine
1 packet (.005 ounce) Italian saffron
1 small cod (¾ pound, approximately)
1 small red snapper (½ pound, approximately)
½ pound halibut steak
½ pound shrimp
2 pounds mussels, cleaned (page 151)
2 tablespoons chopped parsley
4 to 6 slices Italian bread, fried or toasted

Put the olive oil in the bottom of a big, heavy soup pot and sauté the pepper pod in it until dark brown. Discard the pepper and let the oil cool a moment before adding the plum tomatoes. Then raise the heat until the tomatoes start to boil. Lower the heat and simmer for 10 minutes, or until the tomatoes have blended nicely with the oil and the liquid has reduced a bit.

Add the roast pepper strips, the oregano, salt, pepper, and squid. Bring the soup pot to a boil, add the wine, and continue cooking until the wine has evaporated. Cover the pot, lower the heat, and cook for 15 minutes, or until the squid is tender.

In the meantime, chop off the heads and tails of the cod and red snapper, shell the shrimp, and put the fish heads, tails, and the shrimp shells into another pot in water to cover with 1 teaspoon salt. Bring to a boil, cover, lower the heat, and simmer for 15 minutes.

When the squid is tender, cut the cod in half and add it to the soup pot. Strain the broth from the fish heads into the pot. When the pot boils, add the red snapper. When it boils again, add the halibut, return the pot to a boil, lower the heat, and simmer about 5 minutes. The timing here is important: the minute the red snapper and halibut are tender, add the shrimp. As soon as the shrimp are tender, add the mussels and cover the pot. Cook about 3 minutes longer, or until the mussels have opened up.

Sprinkle with the chopped parsley. Serve with the toasted or fried Italian bread. For 4 to 6.

ZUPPA DI RISO, PISELLI, E LATTUGA /
RICE-PEA-LETTUCE SOUP

1 1-pound head romaine lettuce
3 tablespoons unsalted butter
1 tablespoon olive oil
1 10-ounce package frozen peas or 1 pound fresh
3 tablespoons chopped fresh parsley
2 quarts water
2 teaspoons salt
1 cup long-grain rice
4 to 6 tablespoons grated Parmesan cheese

Wash the lettuce thoroughly, discard the thickest of the stems, and chop all the leaves coarsely.

Put the butter and oil into a soup pot over medium heat, add the peas, chopped parsley, and 1 cup of the water, and cook 5 minutes.

Add the chopped lettuce, salt, and the rest of the water. Bring the pot to a boil, add the rice, bring to a boil again, and cook for 14 minutes, or until the rice is tender.

Serve in soup plates, sprinkled with Parmesan cheese as desired. For 6.

ZUPPA DI SPINACI / SPINACH SOUP

2 10-ounce packages fresh spinach
1½ teaspoons salt
4 tablespoons unsalted butter
2 quarts Vegetable Broth (page 97)
3 eggs

4 tablespoons grated Parmesan cheese
½ teaspoon freshly grated nutmeg
6 slices day-old Italian bread (optional), toasted

Wash the spinach thoroughly and put it in a big pot over high heat. Add salt, cover, and cook it, using only the water that clings to the leaves. Stir the spinach a couple of times as it steams. When tender, scoop it into a sieve, saving all the cooking water. As soon as the spinach is cool, squeeze it dry and mince well.

Melt the butter in a frying pan, and sauté the minced spinach in it for 5 minutes. Remove the pan from the heat and let it cool a bit.

Add the vegetable broth to the spinach water and bring to a boil.

Beat the eggs well, and add the Parmesan cheese and nutmeg. Add the minced spinach and mix well.

When the broth boils, pour in the egg-spinach mixture and stir well with a wire whisk. As soon as the soup comes back to a boil, turn off the heat.

Serve with or without toasted slices of Italian bread in the bottom of each soup bowl. For 6 to 8.

RISOTTI / RICE DISHES

Rice, served by itself as a first course, should be cooked with the same care and attention as any good pasta. Like pasta, rice has to be chosen for its quality. It must keep its shape during cooking and when it is served the individual grains should be *al dente,* cooked but firm. It must be capable of taking on flavor as well as giving it.

Italian Arborio rice is the best for any dish — *minestra* or *risotto* — but, not wishing to send anyone to the importers if it can be avoided, we recommend the long-grain rice available in most American grocery stores. For devoted admirers of brown rice, we recommend checking the cooking time of each brand. It usually takes about a third more time to cook brown rice and a third again as much liquid as is required for white rice. We do not recommend the pre-cooked or treated rice that takes a minute to prepare: it cannot give or absorb flavor as well as normal rice, and frequently disintegrates if used in long-cooking dishes.

Traditionally, a good *risotto* is made by sautéing the rice in butter with very finely chopped onion and/or herbs, and then adding only enough liquid to keep it moist as it cooks. As soon as that liquid has been absorbed, a little more is added, and so on until the rice is cooked but *al dente*. This takes up to ½ hour. In experimenting with American rice we have worked out some shorter cooking times. But, in so doing, we have striven for the traditional taste and texture.

Risotto should be served in a shallow soup plate and eaten with a fork, but should be neither soupy nor dry. If in cooking the rice boils too fast it can absorb all the liquid and become dry before it is *al dente,* in which case a little more hot water or a bit of butter must be added to restore the proper amount of moisture and complete the cooking.

RISOTTO ALLA GENOVESE /
RISOTTO WITH TOMATOES AND MUSHROOMS

3 tablespoons unsalted butter
3 tablespoons olive oil
1 garlic clove
1 medium onion
1 pound peeled fresh plum tomatoes
4 fresh basil leaves
½ pound fresh mushrooms
3 tablespoons chopped fresh parsley
2 cups long-grain rice
4¼ cups hot water
4 tablespoons grated Parmesan cheese

Melt 1 tablespoon of the butter in the olive oil in a large saucepan over medium heat. Sauté the garlic in the oil until it is golden, then discard it. Sliver the onion and sauté it in the flavored oil until wilted and translucent but not browned.

Cut the tomatoes into chunks, tear the basil leaves into pieces, and add both to the onion. Boil slowly, stirring occasionally, for 15 to 20 minutes, or until a sauce consistency is reached.

Clean and cut the mushrooms into very thin slices and add to the simmering sauce. Cook over low heat, stirring occasionally, for another 10 minutes, or until the mushrooms are tender but not mushy. Stir in the chopped parsley and cook 2 minutes more.

Cook the rice with the remaining butter and the hot water: bring to a boil, stir the rice, cover the pan, lower the heat, and cook about 10 minutes, or until the rice has absorbed the water and is nearly done. Then add it to the simmering sauce, stir well, and continue cooking uncovered about 4 minutes, or until the rice is *al dente*, tender but firm. Add the Parmesan cheese and stir over low heat for a minute. For 6 to 8.

RISOTTO ALLA PIEMONTESE /
RISOTTO IN RED WINE SAUCE

    1 medium onion, chopped finely
    4 tablespoons unsalted butter
    1 cup dry red wine (Barbera, Barolo, Burgundy)
    2 tablespoons tomato paste, diluted in ½ cup warm water
    2 cups long-grain rice
    1 quart hot Vegetable Broth (page 97) or hot water
    salt to taste
    4 tablespoons grated Parmesan cheese

Sauté the onion in the butter in a soup pot over medium heat until golden and limp, then add ¾ cup of the red wine. When the wine has almost totally evaporated, add the diluted tomato paste. Raise the heat and boil for 3 minutes.

Add the rice, stir well, and keep on cooking. As the rice absorbs the liquid, add a cup or so of the hot broth or water. Continue cooking and adding liquid for 12 minutes, and then add the remaining ¼ cup of red wine. Stir and salt to taste. (If cooking with broth, you may not need any salt; if cooking with water, probably 1½ teaspoons of salt will suit you.) Add more broth (or water) as needed and continue cooking for about 20 minutes or until the rice is *al dente*.

Pour the *risotto* into a heated serving bowl, sprinkle with the Parmesan cheese, stir well, and serve. For 6.

RISOTTO ALLA SICILIANA /
RISOTTO, SICILIAN STYLE

This is a dish whose special style emerges from an uncanny medley of flavorings: vegetable, herb, spice, fruit, and wine. Read about it, make it, and define it for yourself.

SAUCE

3 salted anchovy fillets, or 6 canned
6 tablespoons olive oil
1 large onion
2 tablespoons wine vinegar
½ cup dry white wine
juice of 1½ lemons
1 teaspoon mustard
1 teaspoon salt
freshly ground pepper
4 peeled plum tomatoes, chopped
1 teaspoon dried marjoram leaves
¾ cup pitted Sicilian black olives (packed in brine, not dried)

RICE

2 cups long-grain rice
4 to 4½ cups hot water
2 teaspoons salt

If using salted anchovies, fillet them (page 15); if using canned, drain them. Cook in 3 tablespoons of olive oil in a saucepan over low heat until the anchovies have disintegrated.

Slice the onion into thin slivers and add to the flavored olive oil. Sauté until limp and then add the vinegar. When the vinegar has evaporated, add the wine, lemon juice, mustard, ½ teaspoon of the salt, and pepper (2 or 3 twists of the mill). Stir and cook about 10 minutes.

Put the rice into a heavy pot with 4 cups of the water and the salt. Bring to a boil, stir, cover, lower the heat, and cook for about 14 minutes, or until *al dente*. Stir occasionally during cooking and add a bit more water if necessary.

When the rice is cooked, dress it with the anchovy-wine-sauce and cool slightly.

While the rice is cooling, heat the remaining oil in a frying pan, add the tomatoes, the remaining ½ teaspoon of salt, and the marjoram, and simmer for 10 minutes, stirring constantly.

Pour the tomato sauce over the cooling rice, mix well, decorate with the black olives, and serve. For 6 to 8.

RISOTTO AL POMODORO /
RISOTTO WITH TOMATO SAUCE

    4 tablespoons unsalted butter
    2 cups long-grain rice
    4 cups hot water
    2 teaspoons salt
    1 recipe Basic Tomato Sauce (pages 22–23)
    4 to 6 tablespoons grated Parmesan cheese

Melt the butter in a heavy 3-quart saucepan, add the rice, water, and salt, and bring to a boil. Stir well, cover, lower the heat, and cook for about 8 minutes, stirring occasionally. When almost all of the water has been absorbed, stir in the tomato sauce, and continue to cook uncovered for about 6 minutes, or until the rice is *al dente.* Place in a heated serving dish, sprinkle with the Parmesan cheese, and serve. For 6.

RISOTTO COI TARTUFI / RISOTTO WITH TRUFFLES

This is a dish that deserves perfect rice. If you are unsure of your rice-cooking ability (or your rice, which varies from brand to brand), experiment with other rice dishes before jeopardizing a single truffle.

> 2 cups long-grain rice
> 4¼ cups hot water
> 4 tablespoons unsalted butter
> 2 teaspoons salt
> 4 tablespoons olive oil
> 2 or 3 black truffles (or to taste!)
> 6 tablespoons grated Parmesan cheese

Bring the rice and water to a boil in a heavy 3-quart saucepan along with 2 tablespoons of the butter and the salt. When the rice boils, cover, lower the heat, and continue cooking for about 14 minutes, or until *al dente.* Stir occasionally during cooking.

Meanwhile, cut the truffles paper thin and sauté them in the remaining 2 tablespoons of butter and the olive oil. As soon as the butter and oil begin to sizzle, the truffle "sauce" is ready.

Put the cooked rice into a heated serving bowl, and pour the sauce over it. Add the Parmesan cheese, mix well, and serve. For 6.

RISOTTO CON ASPARAGI /
RISOTTO WITH ASPARAGUS

> 2 pounds fresh asparagus
> 1 large onion
> 5 tablespoons unsalted butter

3 tablespoons olive oil
2 cups long-grain rice
5 cups hot water
3 teaspoons salt
1 packet (.005 ounce) Italian saffron (optional)
4 tablespoons Parmesan cheese, or to taste

Break the root ends off the asparagus stalks where they snap easily and discard. Wash the asparagus thoroughly and cut it into 1-inch pieces.

Finely chop the onion or slice it into thin slivers.

Melt 3 tablespoons of the butter in the olive oil in a big pot over low heat. Add the onion and cook until limp and translucent. Add the asparagus, stir, and cook 2 to 3 minutes.

Add the rice, 4 cups of the hot water, and the salt. Stir well, bring to a boil, cover, lower the heat, and cook for 14 minutes. If you are using saffron, moisten it with 2 tablespoons of the warm water and stir it into the rice.

Keep checking to see that the rice doesn't dry out too much and stir it occasionally. Add some or all of the last cup of hot water as necessary.

When the rice is tender, stir in the remaining 2 tablespoons of butter and the Parmesan cheese. Mix well and serve immediately. Serve extra cheese to sprinkle on according to individual taste. For 6 to 8.

RISO CON L'UVA (ALLA VENETA) /
RICE WITH RAISINS, VENETIAN STYLE

1 cup seedless golden raisins
2 garlic cloves
½ cup chopped fresh parsley
½ cup olive oil
2 cups long-grain rice
1½ teaspoons salt, or to taste

6 to 8 cups boiling water
½ cup grated Parmesan cheese

Soak the raisins in warm water.

Finely chop the garlic with the parsley, and sauté in the olive oil in a big, heavy pot over medium heat for about 5 minutes, or until the parsley is limp.

Add the rice and salt and mix well. Add just enough boiling water to moisten the rice, about 1 cup, and continue cooking over slightly reduced heat. As the water is absorbed, stir in more, about 1 cup at a time, for about 25 minutes, or until the rice is *al dente*.

Remove it from the heat, drain the raisins, and stir them in, together with the cheese. Taste for salt and add some if needed. Serve immediately, with extra grated cheese available for those who want more. For 6.

RISOTO E ZUCHETE DE MAGRO /
RISOTTO WITH ZUCCHINI

In Venetian dialect *risotto* loses a 't' and zucchini becomes *zuchete*. No matter how you spell this dish, it is a favorite of ours. This is the vegetarian version and compares well with any other *risotto*, especially in summer when you can use garden-fresh, small *zuchete*.

1 onion
1 garlic clove
8 tablespoons unsalted butter
5 5-inch zucchini
2½ teaspoons salt
2 cups long-grain rice
4¼ cups hot water
½ cup chopped fresh parsley
freshly ground pepper
4 tablespoons grated Parmesan cheese

Chop the onion with the garlic and sauté them both until barely golden in 6 tablespoons of the butter in a big, heavy soup pot.

Wash the zucchini, cut off the ends, and slice them into very thin rounds. Add the zucchini and ½ teaspoon of the salt to the pot, and sauté until golden over medium heat. Turn the slices frequently so that both sides become equally golden.

Add the rice, the hot water, and the remaining salt. Stir well, cover, and cook for approximately 10 minutes, stirring occasionally.

Uncover the pot, add the remaining butter, parsley, pepper, and cheese, and stir. Continue cooking another 4 minutes, or until the rice is *al dente*. Transfer to a hot serving dish and serve immediately. For 6.

RISO IN BIANCO ALLA SALVIA /
RICE WITH SAGE AND BUTTER

12 tablespoons butter
1 garlic clove
10 leaves fresh sage
2 cups long-grain rice
4 to 4½ cups hot water
2 teaspoons salt
4 to 6 tablespoons grated Parmesan cheese

Melt the butter in a small frying pan over low heat. Split the garlic and chop the sage leaves and add to the melted butter. Cook over very low heat until the garlic is golden and the bits of sage have wilted. Remove from the heat and discard the garlic.

Put the rice in a big pot with 4 cups of water and the salt. Bring to a boil, stir well, cover, lower the heat, and cook about 14 minutes, or until *al dente*, stirring occasionally. If the rice gets dry, add some of the remaining water.

When the rice is cooked, put it into a heated serving dish. Dress with the flavored butter, sprinkle with the Parmesan cheese, and mix well. For 6.

RISOTTO PRIMAVERA /
RISOTTO WITH SPRING VEGETABLES

As its name says, this is a springtime *risotto,* a dish invented to capitalize on the arrival of the new crops in the market. But, out of season, you can evoke a memory of spring: just use frozen vegetables.

1 onion, chopped
1 celery stalk, chopped
3 tablespoons chopped fresh parsley
5 fresh basil leaves
2 tablespoons olive oil
2 tablespoons unsalted butter
½ pound fresh asparagus, or 1 10-ounce package frozen cut
handful of fresh green beans, or ½ 10-ounce package frozen
     whole green beans
3 peeled plum tomatoes, chopped
2 small carrots, diced
2 small potatoes, diced
handful of lettuce leaves, chopped
2 small artichokes, or ½ 9-ounce package frozen artichoke
     hearts
1 pound fresh peas, or 1 10-ounce package frozen peas
4 cups (approximate) hot water
1¾ cups long-grain rice
2½ teaspoons salt
⅓ cup (approximate) grated Parmesan cheese, or to taste

Finely chop together the onion, celery, parsley, and basil and put them in an oven-proof casserole with the butter and olive oil. Sauté over medium heat until the herbs are limp and the bits of onion are barely golden.

If using all fresh vegetables: break off and discard the ends of the asparagus where the stalks snap easily and cut the spears into

1-inch lengths. Cut off the ends of the beans, shell the peas, and slice the artichokes (pages 3–7).

Add the fresh vegetables with the exception of the peas to the sautéed herbs with enough hot water to cover, barely. Bring to a boil, reduce the heat, and simmer for 5 minutes. Add the peas, the rice, the salt, and the remaining hot water. Cover, bring to a boil, lower the heat, and cook, stirring from time to time, for 14 minutes, or until the rice is *al dente*. If during the cooking the rice and vegetables get dry, add a bit more warm water but not enough to make the *risotto* soupy. When the rice is done, stir in the Parmesan cheese and serve immediately.

If using the frozen vegetables: thaw them at room temperature.

Finely chop the herbs and onion and sauté in the butter and oil until limp. Add the carrots, potatoes, lettuce, tomatoes, salt, and water, bring to a boil, lower the heat, cover, and cook about 5 minutes. Cut artichoke hearts in half and add them along with the other thawed vegetables and the rice and continue cooking about 14 minutes, or until the rice is *al dente*. Stir in the Parmesan cheese and serve immediately. For 6 to 8.

RISOTTO VERDE / GREEN RISOTTO

- 1 10-ounce package frozen chopped spinach
- 6 cups boiling water
- 1 medium onion
- 1 small carrot
- 1 celery stalk with leaves
- 8 tablespoons unsalted butter
- 2 cups long-grain rice
- 2 teaspoons salt
- 4 tablespoons freshly chopped parsley
- 4 tablespoons grated Parmesan cheese

Cook the spinach in the boiling water for 3 to 4 minutes, or until completely thawed and tender. Drain the spinach, being careful to save the cooking water. When cool enough to handle, squeeze the spinach dry, again saving the water.

Coarsely chop together the onion, carrot, and celery, and then mix them with the spinach.

Melt the butter in a big, heavy pot over medium heat, add the chopped vegetables but not the parsley, and sauté 15 to 20 minutes, or until limp.

Add the rice, salt, and enough spinach water to cover. Stir, and continue cooking. As the water is absorbed, add more (no more than 1 cup at a time) and continue cooking for about 30 minutes, or until the rice is *al dente*. If the rice absorbs all the spinach water and needs still more liquid, add boiling water as required.

When the rice is cooked, add the chopped parsley and the cheese and stir well. Taste for salt and add some if necessary. Serve immediately. For 6 to 8.

GNOCCHI, TIMBALLI, E AMICI /
DUMPLINGS, CASSEROLES, AND FRIENDS

Because these recipes, though from different families, do all share one common denominator (they take a little more time to put together), we've grouped them under a single heading. They are all good friends, not relatives. There isn't one that won't fit a mood. Just try one when the time feels right.

From the many regional recipes for *gnocchi* (dumplings) we've selected one from Verona in the Veneto and one from Lombardy.

Of the *timballi* (oven-cooked pasta) we include a rich meatless *lasagne* as well as a *polenta* casserole glorified by cheeses and lovingly nicknamed "poor man's *lasagne*." These are generous dishes which serve 8 easily and are good for a crowd.

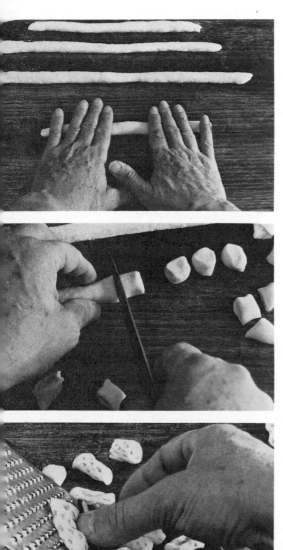

After mixing your dough well, divide it into pieces and roll each piece out with your hands to form sticks of dough no wider than a finger.

With a sharp knife, cut the dough sticks into pieces about 1 inch long.

Press each little piece of dough against the side of a grater. Roll your thumb gently downward and away, letting the dough curl up and be dimpled by the grater.

FILLING
⅔ cup golden seedless raisins
2 10-ounce packages frozen chopped spinach
3 tablespoons (approximate) olive oil
freshly ground pepper
1 teaspoon salt, or to taste

PASTA
2½ cups unbleached all-purpose flour
2 eggs (at room temperature)
½ cup (approximate) milk
vegetable oil for frying

Put the raisins in a cup of warm water to plump up.

Cook the spinach in boiling, salted water until tender (about 5 minutes), drain thoroughly, and, when cool enough to handle, squeeze out as much water as you can with your hands.

Put the spinach and raisins into a bowl, dress with the olive oil, and mix well until the raisins and the spinach are coated with oil and cling together. Add a bit more oil if necessary. Add a few twists of pepper from the mill. Taste for salt and add some if it's needed.

Make a mound of flour on the counter or pastry board, make a well in the center, and break the eggs into it. Add the milk and a pinch of salt. Start stirring with a fork (as you would for pasta, pages 52–53), and then work with your hands to get a smooth, elastic, soft dough. Knead it well and roll it out into a thin sheet as for *fettuccine*. Cut into discs 4 inches in diameter.

Drop a tablespoon or so of the filling on the center of each disc. Moisten the perimeter of each disc with a finger dipped in water and fold it in half, enclosing the filling. Go around the edge of the filled pasta with a fork to seal well. This recipe should make 30 to 36 *cassoni*.

Bring the vegetable oil (1 inch deep) to a high heat in a large frying pan and fry the *cassoni* on both sides to a golden brown. Remove with a slotted spoon and drain briefly on paper towels or brown paper. Serve hot. For 6.

CRESPELLE NAPOLETANE /
NEAPOLITAN CANNELLONI

These *crespelle* (or pancakes), also called *cannelloni,* are made with batter instead of pasta and are covered with sauce either before or after baking, cook's choice. The three main parts of the dish can be made ahead of time and assembled 20 minutes before serving. The recipe doubles easily for a crowd.

CRESPELLE
⅔ cup unbleached all-purpose flour
1 cup milk
1 pinch salt
4 eggs (at room temperature)
2 tablespoons grated Parmesan cheese

FILLING
1 10-ounce package frozen chopped spinach
1 pound *ricotta*
½ teaspoon freshly grated nutmeg

SAUCE
4 tablespoons unsalted butter
2 cups peeled plum tomatoes, chopped
6 or 7 fresh basil leaves
½ teaspoon salt

Make a batter of the flour, milk, salt, eggs, and cheese, and mix well with a wire whisk until smooth. Lightly oil an omelet or frying pan and bring it to medium heat. Spoon in enough batter to cover the bottom of the pan, and cook as you would a pancake, turning when one side is done, removing when both sides are lightly brown and crisp. Add oil as needed to keep the pan lightly coated as you cook successive *crespelle*. (This recipe makes 12 *crespelle* when using an 11-inch omelet pan.) Set them aside to cool while you make the filling.

Cook the frozen spinach in 1 cup boiling salted water until just thawed. Drain in a sieve, squeezing and pressing out as much water as possible. Chop into even finer pieces. Mix the spinach with the *ricotta* and add the nutmeg.

Melt the butter in a saucepan, add the tomatoes, and bring to a boil. Tear the basil leaves into pieces and add to the tomatoes. Lower the heat and simmer 15 minutes, or until the sauce has condensed and darkened in color. Add the salt, stir, taste, and adjust seasonings if necessary.

About ½ hour before serving time, preheat the oven to 300°. Fill the *crespelle* by putting about 4 rounded teaspoons of the spinach-*ricotta* mixture on each one and rolling it up carefully.

If baking with the sauce, cover the bottom of a baking dish with a thin layer of sauce. Arrange the filled *crespelle* on the sauce, packing them close together. Pour the remaining sauce over the *crespelle*.

If you wish crisp *crespelle*, arrange them in a buttered baking dish without sauce and add the sauce after baking.

Bake (at 300°) for 15 minutes, or until heated through. For 6.

GNOCCHI DI PATATE ALLA VERONESE /
POTATO DUMPLINGS FROM VERONA

2 pounds baking potatoes
3 to 3½ cups unbleached all-purpose flour (approximate)
¼ teaspoon salt
6 to 8 tablespoons melted unsalted butter
4 to 6 tablespoons grated Parmesan cheese

Boil the potatoes with their jackets on, drain them the minute they are tender, and peel them as soon as they can be touched. Put them in a big bowl, add the salt, and beat until smooth with an electric beater or mash well with a potato masher.

Add the flour gradually, working it in with a fork. Keep adding flour until you have a workable, rather solid dough.

Generously flour the pastry board or counter and your hands, take a handful of dough, and roll it into a long cylinder no more than ¾ inch in diameter. Cut it into 1-inch slices. Press each slice with your thumb against the side of a cheese grater. Roll your thumb gently downward and away, allowing the dough to curl up a bit and be dimpled by the grater, making a shell-like shape — a *gnoccho*. (See illustration on page 133.) Keep on rolling cylinders, cutting slices, and shaping until all the dough is used. As you finish each *gnoccho,* line it up on a floured cookie sheet. *Gnocchi* should dry at least 2 hours.

When it's time to cook, bring at least 4 quarts of water to a boil in a big pot and add 1 teaspoon of salt for each quart of water. Drop in just enough *gnocchi* to cover the bottom of the pot. As they are done the *gnocchi* rise to the top. Let them cook gently as they float for a minute or two more. Remove with a slotted spoon, drain well over the boiling pot, and put into a warm serving dish. Repeat this process until all the *gnocchi* are cooked. Dress with the melted butter, sprinkle with the cheese, and serve. For 6 to 8.

LASAGNE AL SUGO DI FUNGHI /
LASAGNE WITH MUSHROOM SAUCE

This meatless version of the classic *lasagne* is very light, very delicate, and so special it warrants making homemade pasta. The mushroom sauce by itself can be used with *fettuccine* but when layered with *besciamella,* Parmesan cheese, and egg pasta it has been known to create sheer delight. This is an ideal opportunity for two cooks to operate at the same time.

PASTA
1 4-egg batch *Pasta all'uovo* (pages 47–55)

WHITE SAUCE
1 recipe *Besciamella* (page 20)

MUSHROOM SAUCE
15 parsley sprigs
1 garlic clove
1 5-inch fresh rosemary sprig or 1 teaspoon dried
6 tablespoons unsalted butter
3 tablespoons olive oil
3 cups peeled plum tomatoes
½ cup tomato puree
½ cup water
1 to 1½ pounds big mushrooms, preferably golden
1½ teaspoons salt
¾ cup grated Parmesan cheese

Make the egg pasta, cut it into 4″ x 6″ rectangles (about like pasta post cards), and dry briefly on clean dishtowels or floured cookie sheets.

Make the *besciamella* and let it cool.

Chop the parsley, garlic, and rosemary thoroughly, and sauté them in the butter and olive oil until limp, about 5 minutes. While the herbs are cooking, press down on the bits of garlic with a wooden spoon and mash any resisting pieces to nothingness.

Pass the tomatoes through a food mill and add to the flavored olive oil. Add the tomato puree and water, bring to a boil, lower the heat, and simmer while you prepare the mushrooms.

Clean and slice the mushrooms into ¼-inch thick slices. Add them to the simmering tomatoes. Sprinkle with the salt, stir, cover, and continue cooking about 15 minutes. Taste for salt and add some more if necessary. The sauce at this time should have condensed somewhat, coat the spoon, and be dark in color.

While the sauce is simmering, bring a pot of at least 4 quarts of water to a boil, salt it (1 teaspoon to each quart) and cook the *lasagne* a few at a time. Using a slotted spoon, remove the *lasagne* when they have floated to the top and are *al dente* (each batch takes about 5 minutes). Drain them in a colander, and then run cold water over them to prevent sticking and stop further cooking.

While you preheat the oven to 350°, the assembling process may begin. Coat the bottom of a *lasagne* baking dish (14" x 10" x 3") with a very thin layer of mushroom sauce, 2 or 3 tablespoons. Cover with a layer of *lasagne*. Add another thin layer of sauce, then form a layer of *besciamella* by evenly spacing tablespoonsful of the white sauce about 2 inches apart. Sprinkle with some Parmesan cheese. Add another layer of pasta. Continue until all the ingredients are used up, aiming to finish with a layer of Parmesan. Tuck the pasta in all around the edges.

Bake (at 350°) for about 30 minutes. Cool for 15 minutes before cutting. For 8.

STROZZAPRETI / SWISS CHARD DUMPLINGS

The name *strozzapreti*, priest-chokers, which appears in practically every region of Italy (this recipe is from Lombardy), describes a variety of different dishes. The name perhaps is part of the same folklore as *il boccone del Curato*, the curate's morsel. In small villages at harvest time it was traditional to give the curates special presents, dishes made with the best of the crop. Naturally, curates developed a taste for excellence. This particular dish is so good that a curate would be likely to devour it with such gusto that he might well choke himself.

2 pounds Swiss chard
3 eggs
1 cup grated Parmesan cheese
8 tablespoons unsalted butter
1 cup fine bread crumbs (approximate)

Wash the chard very carefully, drain it, discard the coarsest stems, and cut the remaining stems and leaves into 5-inch lengths. Cook the chard in boiling salted water until very tender. Drain thoroughly in a colander and, when it is cool enough to handle, squeeze it dry. Chop the drained chard as finely as possible.

Put the chopped chard in a big bowl and mix in the eggs with a fork. Add ¾ cup of the cheese, mix again, and let the mixture sit for a few minutes.

Stir in enough bread crumbs to make a soft dough, thick enough to stick together and form a small ball about the size of a cherry when rolled between the palms of the hands. Roll all of the mixture into little balls, lining them up on a cookie sheet as they are finished.

Bring at least 4 quarts of water to a boil in a large pot, and salt it with 1 teaspoon of salt per quart of water. Cook the dumplings a few at a time, adding just enough to cover the bottom of the pot. As they cook, they rise to the top. Let them float a minute or two and then remove them with a slotted spoon to a hot serving dish and keep warm. Dot with butter. Keep on cooking and buttering until all are done. Sprinkle with the remaining cheese and serve immediately. For 6.

SUPPLÌ DI MAGRO / RICE CROQUETTES

This is a grand way to serve rice for a snack or a *contorno*. It is also an excellent way to use leftover *risotto*.

> 1 recipe cold *risotto* (pages 123, 125, 127, 129)
> 1 egg
> 1 teaspoon freshly grated nutmeg
> ¼ pound whole-milk *mozzarella* (Swiss or Muenster cheese may be substituted), cut in ½-inch cubes
> 1 cup unseasoned bread crumbs
> vegetable oil for frying

Put the *risotto* in a bowl, add the egg and nutmeg, and mix well.

Scoop out enough rice to fill your cupped hand. Put a cube of cheese in the center of the hand-held rice (it will be the core of the *supplì*). Compress and gently shape the rice into a cylinder with rounded ends. Roll it in bread crumbs and set it aside. Continue scooping and shaping until all the mixture has been transformed into about 16 to 20 generous *supplì*.

Put ½ inch of vegetable oil into a large frying pan over high heat. When the oil is hot, use a slotted spoon to lower the *supplì* into it, putting in as many as will fit comfortably. Once one side has browned nicely, turn the *supplì* carefully and fry the other side. When evenly brown and crisp all around, remove with slotted spoon and drain on absorbent paper. Serve warm. *Supplì* can be reheated easily in an oven if you wish to make them ahead of serving time. For 8.

TIMBALLO DI MACCHERONI E MELANZANE /
MACARONI-AND-EGGPLANT CASSEROLE

3 to 4 (about 2½ pounds) medium-sized eggplants
vegetable oil for frying
1 medium onion
1 garlic clove
7 tablespoons unsalted butter
3 cups peeled plum tomatoes, chopped
10 fresh basil leaves
1 teaspoon salt, or to taste
1 pound macaroni (*ziti* or *mostaccioli*)
½ cup bread crumbs
½ pound Provolone cheese, thinly sliced

Slice the eggplants lengthwise into ½-inch slices and prepare as usual (pages 7–9). Afterward dry the slices with paper towels and fry them in vegetable oil until golden brown on both sides. Drain on paper towels or brown paper.

Slice the onion into thin slivers. Melt all but 1 tablespoon of the butter in a big frying pan over medium heat, add the onion and the garlic clove, and sauté until the onion is limp and translucent.

Add the tomatoes to the onion. Tear the basil leaves into pieces, and add them and the salt to the tomatoes. When the pan comes to a boil, cover it, lower the heat, and simmer for 20 minutes, or until a good sauce consistency has been reached. Stir occasionally as the sauce simmers.

Remove the garlic clove from the sauce before assembling the casserole.

Cook the pasta in the usual fashion (pages 56–58). After draining it, run cold water over it to cool it, prevent it from sticking together, and stop the cooking process. Let the cold water drain off.

While you are preheating the oven to 350°, butter a 4-quart, round oven-proof bowl with the last of the butter. Sprinkle the buttered bowl with some of the bread crumbs to coat the entire inside.

Put a layer of pasta in the bottom of the bowl. Add 4 to 5 tablespoons of sauce and cover with fried eggplant.

Add a layer of cheese to the casserole.

Continue layering until all the ingredients are used (makes 3 or 4 layers), aiming to finish with a layer of cheese. Sprinkle with the remaining bread crumbs.

Bake (at 350°) for 20 to 30 minutes, or until toasted on top and hot through. For 6 to 8.

TIMBALLO DI RIGATONI, FORMAGGIO, E PISELLI / MACARONI CASSEROLE WITH CHEESE AND PEAS

1 recipe *Besciamella* (page 20)
½ onion
4 tablespoons unsalted butter
1 10-ounce package frozen peas or ¾ pound fresh
½ teaspoon salt

¼ pound Fontina or Muenster cheese, diced
½ cup unseasoned bread crumbs
1 pound macaroni (*rigatoni, mostaccioli, ziti*)
4 tablespoons grated Parmesan cheese

Preheat the oven to 350°.

Prepare the *besciamella* and set aside to cool.

Cut the onion into very thin slices, and sauté in 3 tablespoons of the butter until wilted and translucent. Add the peas and salt and cook 5 minutes, or until the peas are tender. If using fresh peas, you may have to add a bit of water before they are tender, depending on how big the peas are and how long off the vine.

Cook the pasta (pages 56–58) and drain immediately. Then run cold water over the pasta in the colander to cool it, prevent stickiness, and stop further cooking.

Mix together the drained pasta, cheese, and onion-flavored peas.

Butter a round, oven-proof 4-quart bowl with the remaining tablespoon of butter. Sprinkle the buttered bowl with about 1 tablespoon of the bread crumbs, turning the dish around and about to make the crumbs cling evenly.

Spoon a layer of the pasta mixture into the bottom of the bowl. Dot with tablespoons of *besciamella,* and sprinkle with some of the Parmesan cheese.

Continue layering until all the ingredients are used, but make sure to end with the *besciamella* on top. Mix the last of the Parmesan cheese with the remaining bread crumbs and sprinkle on top of the casserole.

Bake (at 350°) for 20 to 30 minutes, or until the casserole is toasted on top.

Cool for 15 minutes and serve. If you cool the *timballo* longer, you should be able to turn it out on a serving plate without its falling apart. For 6 to 8.

POLENTA

There's no way to translate the name of this staple of northern Italy. *Polenta* is simply *polenta*. It is used for almost any course in a meal, or as a snack. Made of cornmeal boiled in salted water, by itself it is rather uninteresting, but when served with a sauce or in a casserole, *polenta* is as appetizing as any dish of pasta.

> 2 cups fine cornmeal
> 10 cups water
> 3 teaspoons salt

Bring 5 cups of water to a boil in a big pot over high heat. Mix the cornmeal in the remaining cold water, stirring rapidly. When smooth, pour the cold mixture slowly into the boiling water. Add the salt. Bring back to a boil, lower the heat almost to a simmer, and cook for 50 to 60 minutes, stirring almost constantly (*polenta*-making requires endurance), especially after it comes back to a boil. When cooked, *polenta* should be thick, smooth, and creamy. For 6.

TIMBALLO DI POLENTA / POLENTA CASSEROLE

This is an Alpine specialty, also called *Polenta pastisada,* which is sometimes referred to as Poor Man's *Lasagne.* Quite frankly, there are quite a few runners-up for that coveted title, but this one, rich in sauce and cheese, is a leading contender.

> POLENTA
> 1½ cups fine cornmeal
> 7½ cups water
> 2 teaspoons salt
>
> SAUCE
> 6 tablespoons unsalted butter

½ pound peeled plum tomatoes
1 pound large mushrooms, preferably golden
½ pound whole-milk *mozzarella,* shredded
4 tablespoons grated Parmesan cheese

Make the *polenta* (page 144) using the above proportions of corn-meal to water. Once cooked, pour it onto a board or clean counter, spread it to form a layer about ½ inch thick, and let it cool.

Preheat the oven to 350°.

Melt the butter in a large saucepan over medium heat.

Pass the tomatoes through a sieve or food mill, and add them to the butter. Add the salt. Cook and stir for 5 minutes at a brisk boil.

Cut the mushrooms into thin slices, and add them to the tomato sauce. Lower the flame and cook about 5 minutes more, or until the mushrooms are barely limp.

Coat the bottom of a 3 to 4 quart oven-proof casserole with a few tablespoons of sauce but no mushrooms. Cut the cold *polenta* into shapes to fit the casserole. Spread a layer of *polenta* in the bottom of the casserole. Spoon on enough mushroom-tomato sauce to cover, and sprinkle with shredded or grated *mozzarella.*

Continue layering, spooning, sprinkling until all the ingredients are used, aiming to end with a layer of sauce.

Sprinkle with the Parmesan cheese and bake (at 350°) for 25 to 30 minutes. Serve warm. For 6 to 8.

POLENTA CONCIA (O AI QUATTRO FORMAGGI) / POLENTA WITH FOUR CHEESES

This is a northern Italian dish from the Val d'Aosta where it is served hot in the winter as a first course or cold as an accompaniment to second courses, taking the place of bread.

POLENTA
1½ cups fine cornmeal

7½ cups water
2 teaspoons salt

1 cup milk
4 tablespoons unsalted butter
¼ pound Muenster cheese
¼ pound Swiss cheese
¼ pound sharp Cheddar cheese
4 tablespoons grated Parmesan cheese

Make *polenta* (page 144) using the above proportions of corn-meal to water.

While the *polenta* is cooking, cube the cheeses. When the *polenta* is ready, add the milk, and bring the pot back to a boil, stirring constantly. Cook for 5 minutes.

Add the butter and cubed cheeses and continue stirring and cooking until the cheese has melted.

Pour the *polenta* onto a lightly buttered platter, sprinkle with the Parmesan cheese, let cool 10 minutes, and serve. For 6 to 8.

SECONDI PIATTI

SECOND COURSES

WRITING ABOUT meatless second courses after a collection of soups, pasta, and rice dishes is like answering the age-old question, "What do you do for an encore?"

Second courses should balance the ingredients, taste, and texture of whatever has gone before. In *cucina di magro,* the second course has for centuries leaned hard on fish and eggs. In meatless menus to fit today's mood, traditional Italian casseroles, in which vegetables combine to make a substantial dish, supplement the more familiar *secondi piatti.*

The fish dishes are mostly combinations of fish and seasonings common to most American markets. While in parts of the country that are some distance from the sea fresh fish is rather a luxury, quick-frozen fish can generally be found in any market, and old favorites such as salt cod and canned tuna also come to the rescue: cod in a sauce, tuna as a staple in stuffings for vegetables.

As for eggs, Italy gets a lot of mileage from *frittate,* or omelets, and from casseroles in which eggs share the honors with vegetables. They are also served all by themselves, or poached in a simple sauce, but *never* for breakfast.

PESCE / FISH

As is characteristic of all Italian cooking, geography and economy both contribute to Italians' love of fish and their ingenuity in using it. Nearly every region of the peninsula touches the sea, and areas that don't are blessed with large and fishable lakes. Every region has its own way of cooking either fresh or salt water fish, one that is compatible with local markets and tastes.

A complete discussion of Italian (that is, Mediterranean) fish would take a book. Above and beyond the species common to most areas, some Italian regions have their very own native fish. To confuse the issue, sometimes the same fish is given different names in different regions. And the same is true of the recipes. The main thing to know is that Mediterranean fish do have cousins in the Atlantic and Pacific oceans and that genealogical distinctions, once a fish is in the pan, can be overlooked.

To be perfectly frank, Italians treat their fish no differently from fish lovers the world over. In short, they do not overcook or overseason.

General Advice

If you find fresh fish in the market, snap them up.

Do not discard heads and tails; they add flavor when poaching, preserve shape when grilling.

When using frozen fish, thaw it on the least cold shelf of the refrigerator.

When buying frozen shrimp, choose the ones that have not been shelled.

If you have a choice, buy the smallest squid.

SALT COD: either in its Italian form (beheaded, opened flat, salted, and dried stiff as a board) or in filleted form (skinned, boned, and boxed) it needs a long soaking: 12 to 24 hours in fresh water, changed as many times as possible, until the fish is plump again and has lost most of its saltiness.

TUNA: as for canned tuna, try to get Italian brands which are packed in olive oil (pages 15–16).

SQUID: In most markets squid, whether fresh or frozen, has to be cleaned by the buyer. The procedure is simple.

Remove the tentacles by cutting between them and the eyes. With your fingers pop out the mouth which is hidden in the center of the tentacles and discard it. Reserve the tentacles.

Hold the squid under running water and with one hand squeeze the body or mantle, and with the other pull off and discard the head and with it the attached innards. Peel off the mantle's thin reddish outer membrane. Rinse the inside of the mantle and pull out and discard its transparent quill-like bone.

MUSSELS: To clean mussels: scrub the shells under running water with a very stiff brush, pull off any fibers, barnacles, or algae that may remain, and squeeze each mussel hard to make sure that it's tightly closed or that it closes up immediately. If opened slightly, a live one will fight back and close. If a mussel remains open and won't shut, throw it away.

Rinse the cleaned mussels carefully before cooking as directed. If on cooking a mussel does not open, discard it; it was probably dead before cooking and is thus suspect.

Boning Fish

When it comes to boning fish after cooking, there are more novices and self-educated cooks than professional ones. In the hope of helping the first two categories, here are a few techniques and rules that have worked well for us:

Skin a fish while it is still warm.

When boning a fish, begin by completing the slit on the underside, cutting in to the backbone. Make a similar slit along the top (dorsal fin) side of the fish. Cut the flesh down to the backbone behind the head and before the tail. Slide a fish knife between the backbone and the flesh and lift off the top fillet. In

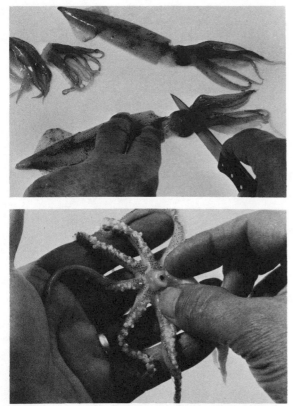

Remove the tentacles by cutting between them and the eyes.

With your fingers pop out the mouth which is hidden in the center of the tentacles and discard it. Reserve the tentacles

Hold the squid under running water and with one hand squeeze the body or mantle and with the other pull off and discard the head and with it the attached innards.

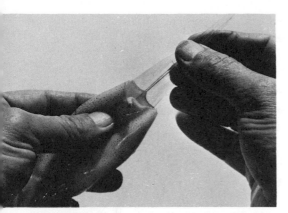

Pull out and discard the transparent quill-like bone.

Peel off the mantle's thin reddish outer membrane.

Cut the body in rings. Leave the tentacles whole or, if very large, cut them in half.

large fish, it is easier to lift the fillet in two sections, separating it along the natural division that runs down the middle of the fish, head to tail. Take hold of the tail and lift out the backbone and the head. Remove the fine bones from the edges of the fillet.

You can use the same technique with raw fish, but you must use a very sharp knife to cut the flesh gently from the bone and to cut the bones themselves.

ARAGOSTA BOLLITA / BOILED LOBSTER

Like shrimp, boiled lobsters are served about the same way on both sides of the ocean, simply with lemon and oil or homemade *maionese*.

3 1-pound lobsters
9 quarts water
6 teaspoons salt
1 onion
1 carrot
10 parsley sprigs
1 celery stalk with leaves
½ cup wine vinegar
1½ lemons, cut into wedges
olive oil, or 1 recipe *Maionese* (pages 20–21)

Bring the water to a boil and add the salt and seasonings. When it boils again put in as many lobsters as will fit comfortably. If cooking more than 3 lobsters at a time, adjust the recipe accordingly. Bring back to a boil, lower the heat to a gentle boil, and cook the lobsters 6 minutes. Remove from the water and put them on a platter to drain.

With a very sharp knife, cut the lobsters open on the underside from head to tail. Crack the claws, and let as much water as possible drain out. Place on a serving platter. Serve with lemon wedges and good olive oil or with *maionese*. For 3.

BACCALÀ ALLA NAPOLETANA /
SALT COD, NEAPOLITAN STYLE

1 pound salt cod fillets
flour
vegetable oil for frying
3 tablespoons olive oil
2 garlic cloves
1 red pepper pod, seeded, or ¼ teaspoon Tabasco sauce
⅓ cup black Sicilian olives (packed in brine, not dried)
1 tablespoon capers
3 cups peeled plum tomatoes, chopped
freshly ground pepper to taste
3 tablespoons chopped fresh parsley

Soak the cod for 12 to 24 hours (page 150).

When the cod has soaked and lost its saltiness, drain it well and cut it into pieces about 3" x 4". Dredge the pieces in flour, patting both sides to get as much flour to stick as possible. Bring the vegetable oil to high heat and brown the cod thoroughly on both sides. Drain and cool on paper towels.

Put the olive oil in a wide saucepan or a frying pan big enough to hold the fried fish pieces in one layer if possible. Sauté the garlic and red pepper in the olive oil until golden and brown and then discard them. Let the oil cool down a bit.

Drain and pit the olives and rinse off the capers. Mince these two together. Add the tomatoes, capers, and olives to the flavored olive oil, stir well, and return to a boil. Lower the heat and simmer for 10 minutes. Add the fried cod and simmer, again for 10 minutes.

Taste for salt; it shouldn't need any, but it might. Add freshly ground pepper to taste and continue simmering for another 10 minutes. Sprinkle with parsley and serve. For 6.

BACCALÀ ALLA PIZZAIOLA /
SALT COD IN PIZZA SAUCE

  1 pound salt cod fillets
  3 tablespoons olive oil
  2 garlic cloves
  3 cups peeled plum tomatoes
  1½ teaspoons oregano
  freshly ground pepper

Soak the cod (page 150) and then drain it on paper towels, pat dry, and cut into 3″ x 4″ pieces.

In a pan large enough to hold all the fish in one layer, sauté the garlic in the olive oil until golden and discard. Let the oil cool a moment. Cut the tomatoes into chunks and add to the frying pan along with the oregano and pepper (5 or 6 twists of the mill). Stir, bring to a boil, and then simmer for 5 minutes.

Add the cod to the sauce and cook at a gentle boil covered for 10 minutes and uncovered for another 10 minutes, or until the cod flakes easily. Serve hot with Italian bread or mashed potatoes. For 6.

BRANZINO ALLA BRACE /
GRILLED STRIPED BASS OR ROCKFISH

This is a good way to marinate other fish similar to the striped bass such as perch, red snapper, even the humble rose fish. If larger than 2 pounds, double the marinade.

  1 2-pound striped bass or rockfish
  2 lemons
  ½ cup dry sherry
  ½ cup olive oil
  1 fresh rosemary sprig or 2 teaspoons dried
  ½ teaspoon salt

3 to 4 drops Tabasco sauce, or ½ red pepper pod, seeded
pinch of sugar

Have the fish cleaned (or do it yourself), but leave the head and
tail on.

Squeeze 1 lemon and mix the juice with the sherry and all the
other ingredients in a bowl. If using the red pepper pod, break it
up in pieces before adding to the marinade.

Put the fish in a suitable deep dish and pour the marinade in.
Let the fish marinate for at least 1 hour, turning it over a few
times. While the fish marinates, start your grill.

When the coals are ready, oil the grill, and set it about 4 inches
above the coals. Take the fish out of the marinade and put it on
the grill. Cook each side until the skin blisters and crackles, brushing frequently with the marinade.

When the fish is done, remove it to a platter, skin and bone it,
and serve with the remaining lemon cut in wedges and a dribble
of good olive oil. For 4.

CUSCUSU / COUS-COUS, SICILIAN STYLE

Originally an Arab dish, this is one of several Sicilian variations
in which semolina, steamed with spices, is served with fish broth,
tomatoes, and fish. Its taste is as far removed from the North
African cous-cous as the time of the first Arab invasion of Sicily is
from today, and that's six centuries more or less.

COUS-COUS
1 pound semolina flour, or 1 pound packaged cous-cous
1 packet (.005 ounce) Italian saffron, diluted in ⅓ cup warm
   water
2 tablespoons olive oil
½ teaspoon salt
½ teaspoon cinnamon

3 pounds fresh fish, as varied as possible (halibut, porgy,
   ½ pound mussels, ½ pound shrimp, whitefish, butterfish,
   to name a few)
1 large onion
½ red pepper pod, seeded
½ cup olive oil
¾ cup almonds
4 garlic cloves
2 tablespoons chopped fresh parsley
2 cups plum tomatoes, chopped
1 teaspoon ground white pepper
3 quarts warm water
2 teaspoons salt, or to taste

If using semolina flour: mix the saffron with the warm water. Put
1 or 2 tablespoons of the saffron water in a large, shallow earthenware bowl and tilt the bowl to dampen the sides thoroughly. With
one hand sift the semolina flour into the bowl, and with the fingertips of the other hand mix it swiftly to obtain small lumps of
cous-cous no bigger than grains of rice. Once you have obtained
the grains, put them to dry on a clean kitchen towel or brown
paper (clean paper bags are fine for this). Continue until all the
flour is dampened and then let dry for 30 minutes. Once dry, mix
it with the 2 tablespoons of oil, the salt, and the cinnamon. Steam
the semolina in a cous-cous steamer or rice steamer for 1½ hours.

If using packaged cous-cous: mix it well with the olive oil, cinnamon, salt, and saffron diluted in 2 tablespoons warm water. Steam
it in a cous-cous steamer or rice steamer for 1½ hours.

While the cous-cous steams, prepare the fish broth. Clean the
fish, and save the heads and the shrimp shells. Slice the onion into
slivers, and sauté it gently with the red pepper pod in a large pot
with the olive oil.

Pound together in a mortar the almonds, garlic, and chopped
parsley. Add to the onion, and stir and cook gently for 2 to 3
minutes. Add the chopped tomatoes and the white pepper. Cook
for a moment or two, or until all the ingredients have blended.

Add the warm water and salt, and bring to a boil. Once the broth is boiling, add the fish heads and shrimp shells, and cook 20 minutes. If using mussels, clean them well (page 151), add them to the soup, and boil them until they have opened. Retrieve the mussels with a slotted spoon and put them aside for later use. When the broth has cooked, put it through a sieve into another pot and keep warm over a low heat. Discard the fish heads and shrimp shells.

As soon as the cous-cous is steamed, put it into a warmed earthenware bowl and pour just enough fish broth over to cover and keep warm. Put in the fish along with the remaining broth, according to texture, the meatier fish first. When the broth reaches a boil, add the more delicate fish. Keep the broth boiling gently until the fish is done. (The fleshier fish take about 20 minutes in all and the smaller fish 14, while the shrimp are done in 4 to 5 minutes.) Take care not to overcook. When all the fish are about a minute away from being cooked, add the mussels in order to reheat them.

Put the fish and its broth in a soup tureen but leave the cous-cous in its bowl. Serve the cous-cous, adding some fish and some broth to each plate, as you please. For 8.

CUSCUSU CU E COZZE /
COUS-COUS WITH MUSSELS

COUS-COUS
1 pound semolina flour, or 1 pound packaged cous-cous
3 tablespoons olive oil
1 packet (.005 ounce) Italian saffron, diluted in ⅓ cup warm water
½ teaspoon cinnamon
1 teaspoon salt

BROTH
2 onions
½ cup olive oil

1 red pepper pod, seeded
4 garlic cloves
¾ cup almonds
4 tablespoons chopped fresh parsley
3 tablespoons tomato paste, diluted in ¾ cup warm water
3 teaspoons salt
3 pounds fish heads, cheeks, tails
2¾ quarts warm water
3 to 3½ pounds mussels

Prepare the cous-cous as in the preceding recipe (page 158).

While the semolina steams, prepare the fish broth. Cut the onions into thin slivers and sauté in a big soup pot over medium heat along with the garlic cloves and red pepper pod until the garlic is golden, the pepper pod dark brown. Discard the garlic and pepper. Chop the almonds and 2 tablespoons of the parsley into a paste, using either a blender or a good sharp knife followed up by a mortar and pestle. Add to the soup pot, and stir and cook gently for 2 to 3 minutes. Add the diluted tomato paste. Simmer until all the ingredients are well integrated. Add the salt, fish heads, cheeks, tails, and 2¾ quarts water. Bring the pot to a boil, cover, lower the heat, and simmer for at least 40 minutes. Taste for salt after about 20 minutes and add more if needed.

While the broth cooks and the cous-cous steams, clean the mussels (page 151).

When the broth is done, strain it through a sieve into a clean pot.

When the cous-cous is cooked, remove it from the top section of the steamer and put it into a big bowl. Pour enough fish broth onto the semolina to cover. Cover the bowl and keep in a warm place for 20 minutes.

Bring the remaining broth to a boil, add the mussels, and cook covered for 5 minutes, or until the mussels are open.

Serve the cous-cous from the big bowl and the mussels and fish broth from a soup tureen. Let each person add more broth and mussels to his serving of cous-cous as he wishes. For 8.

MERLUZZO ALLA SICILIANA /
FISH FILLETS IN ANCHOVY SAUCE

2 pounds fresh fillets of hake, cod, haddock, or whiting
2 large eggs
½ cup (approximate) all-purpose flour
1 cup (approximate) unseasoned bread crumbs
6 salted anchovies or 12 canned fillets
6 tablespoons olive oil
vegetable oil for frying
3 tablespoons chopped fresh parsley
1½ lemons

If the fish fillets are unmanageably long (more than 7 or 8 inches), cut them in half.

Beat the eggs until they are light in color and foamy.

Put the flour on one plate and the bread crumbs on another. Dredge the fillets in flour, pat them well to shake off any extra flour which doesn't adhere, dip them in the beaten eggs, and finally press them into the bread crumbs, first one side and then the other, and pat well. Set aside.

Prepare (page 15) and mince the anchovies. Warm the olive oil in a small saucepan over low heat and add the minced anchovies. Cook, stirring constantly, until the anchovies have disintegrated. (Do not overheat as the anchovy bits will just fry.) Once the mixture looks like a sauce, which usually occurs after about 5 minutes, set it aside in a warm place.

Heat the vegetable oil to 375°, or medium heat, in a big frying pan and sauté the fish fillets on both sides to a golden brown. (If the oil isn't hot enough, the fillets just absorb it and become soggy; if too hot, the oil tends to darken the bread crumbs and egg coating too much before the inner fish is cooked.)

When the fish fillets are nicely browned on both sides, remove them and put them on absorbent paper to drain.

Once all the fish is cooked, place it on a warm serving platter. Add the parsley to the anchovy sauce, stir, and pour it over the fillets. Serve with lemon wedges. For 4 to 6.

PESCE ALL'ANCONETANA /
FRIED FISH IN TOMATO SAUCE FROM ANCONA

FISH
2 to 2½ pounds pollock, fresh cod, salt cod fillets (page 150)
flour
vegetable oil for frying

SAUCE
3 garlic cloves
4 tablespoons olive oil
3 cups peeled plum tomatoes
3 tablespoons chopped fresh parsley
½ teaspoon salt
freshly ground pepper to taste

Cut the fish in pieces approximately 2″ x 3″, dredge them in flour, wait 5 to 10 minutes, and then dredge them again, patting the flour on well.

Put at least 1 inch of vegetable oil in a frying pan and bring it to 375°, or medium heat. Fry the fish pieces a few at a time until both sides are golden brown. Then let them drain on absorbent paper. Keep them in a warm place while making the sauce.

In a saucepan, sauté the garlic in the olive oil until golden, and then discard the cloves. Let the flavored oil cool a bit.

Put the tomatoes through a food mill or coarse sieve, add them to the cooling olive oil, and bring the pan back to a boil, stirring as it heats. Add the parsley, the salt, and pepper (a few twists of the mill), lower the heat, and simmer the sauce for about 15 to 20 minutes, or until it has reduced somewhat and darkened in color.

Put the fried fish pieces on a serving platter, cover them with sauce, and serve immediately. For 4 to 6.

PESCE ALLA GRIGLIA CON SALSA VERDE /
GRILLED FISH WITH GREEN SAUCE

4 pounds (approximate) whole fish (red snapper, sea bass, rock fish, porgy, or any fish that grills well)
1 recipe *Salsa verde* (pages 23–24)
¼ cup (approximate) olive oil

Start the charcoal grill.

Clean the fish, but leave the heads and tails intact.

Spread about 1 teaspoon of *salsa verde* in each fish cavity (enough to moisten the insides).

When the coals of the grill are ready, brush both sides of the fish with olive oil and put them on the grill. Turn when the first side is done and grill the second side. Brush with olive oil as the fish cooks.

Serve with the remaining *salsa verde*. For 6.

PESCE ALLA ROMAGNOLA /
FISH IN WHITE SAUCE

1 2- to 2½-pound whole fish (sea bass or red snapper)
salt to taste
6 tablespoons unsalted butter
1 cup dry white wine
½ recipe *Besciamella* (page 20)
½ cup (approximate) unseasoned bread crumbs
juice of ½ lemon

Scale and clean the fish. Cut off the head and tail. Sprinkle the inside and outside of the fish lightly with salt.

Melt 4 tablespoons of the butter in a pan large enough to hold the fish. Sauté the fish briefly on both sides. Add the wine, lower the heat to simmer, cover the pan, and cook for 10 minutes, or until the fish is barely done.

Lift the fish out of its pan and remove the skin while it is still warm. Let the fish cool.

Preheat the oven to 375°.

While the fish is cooling, prepare the *besciamella,* cooking it until it is nice and thick.

Bone the fish.

Lightly butter an oven-proof casserole, sprinkle with about 2 tablespoons of bread crumbs, and put half the *besciamella* in the bottom of the casserole. Reassemble the fish on top of the white sauce.

Add the lemon juice to the liquid in the poaching pan, stir, and boil it down a bit. Pour a few spoonfuls over the fish just to moisten it. Cover with the last of the *besciamella.* Sprinkle with bread crumbs. Dot with the remaining 2 tablespoons of butter. Bake the casserole (at 375°) until the butter has melted and the bread crumbs have toasted. For 4.

PESCE BOLLITO CON SALSA VERDE /
POACHED FISH WITH GREEN SAUCE

1 4- to 5-pound whole fresh fish (whitefish, small cod, hake, striped bass, pollock, haddock, red or rose fish, red snapper, sea bass) or large fish steaks such as halibut
10 parsley sprigs
1 fresh rosemary sprig
1 celery stalk with leaves
1 bay leaf
1 medium onion, quartered
1 lemon, quartered
6 teaspoons salt
10 peppercorns
3 cups dry white wine, or ¾ cup wine vinegar
1 recipe *Salsa verde* (pages 23–24)

Have the fish cleaned (or do it yourself), but leave the head and tail on for added flavor. Wrap it in kitchen cheesecloth so that it can be easily removed from its pan when cooked.

Put the fish in a fish poacher (for lack of one, you can use a roasting pan). Add the herbs, celery, onion, lemon, wine or vinegar. Add enough cold water just to cover the fish. Cover the pan, bring to a boil over medium heat, lower the heat, and simmer about 5 minutes to the pound, or until the flesh breaks open easily when pierced with a fork.

While the fish is poaching, make a recipe of *salsa verde*.

When the fish is cooked, lift it out of its broth, skin it, bone it, and put the two fillets (side by side or one on top of the other) on a serving platter. Cover with *salsa verde* and serve with remaining sauce. For 6.

PESCE 'MBRIACO / FISH IN WINE SAUCE

'Mbriaco is dialect for someone who has imbibed too much wine. These fish steaks use less than a glass of *vino* which in cooking is transformed into a delicate sauce.

2 pounds fish steaks (swordfish, tuna, halibut), no more than
   1 inch thick
1 onion
6 parsley sprigs
1 garlic clove
5 tablespoons olive oil
¾ cup dry red wine
1 tablespoon unbleached all-purpose flour, dissolved in ¼
   cup cold water
½ teaspoon salt

Chop together finely the onion and garlic. Sauté them with the parsley in olive oil in a pan large enough to hold the fish steaks in one layer. When the chopped seasonings are limp and the parsley bits have darkened, add the fish steaks and sauté them a few minutes on each side until whitened.

Add the wine, raise the heat, and as the wine evaporates add the flour and water. Add the salt, and push the steaks back and forth to mix the sauce evenly. Cover the pan, lower the heat, and cook 10 minutes, or until the fish flesh breaks open easily when pierced with a fork. Serve immediately with hot Italian bread. For 4 to 6.

SCAMPI BOLLITI / BOILED SHRIMP

2½ pounds fresh shrimp (or frozen with the shell on)
2 quarts boiling water
2 teaspoons salt
1 onion
1 carrot
10 parsley sprigs
1 celery stalk
1 bay leaf
¼ cup wine vinegar
1 recipe *Maionese* (pages 20–21), or 2 to 3 tablespoons olive oil and 1½ lemons, cut into wedges

Shell and devein the shrimp.

Bring the water to a boil, and add all the seasonings including the vinegar but use the stems of the parsley only, reserving the leaves. Bring the water back to a boil, add the shrimp, bring to a boil again, lower the heat, and cook 3 minutes. Remove from the heat, let stand a moment or two, drain, and discard the seasonings.

Chop the parsley leaves. Put the shrimp in a serving dish, sprinkle with the minced parsley, and toss.

Serve with *maionese,* or dribble the olive oil over the shrimp, toss, and serve while still warm with the lemon wedges. For 6.

SEPPIE IN ZIMINO / SQUID WITH SWISS CHARD

3 pounds small squid, fresh or frozen
1 onion
¾ cup chopped fresh parsley
1 celery stalk
4 tablespoons olive oil
2 pounds Swiss chard
⅔ cup crushed plum tomatoes
freshly ground pepper
1½ to 2 teaspoons salt, or to taste

Clean the squid and cut the tentacles in half lengthwise, the body in rings (pages 151–153).

Chop the onion, parsley, and celery together, and sauté in olive oil in a soup pot for 3 or 4 minutes or until golden green.

Wash the chard thoroughly (at least 3 changes of water) to get rid of all possible sand or soil. Discard the toughest stems, using only the tender ones, cut the chard into big chunks, and add to the herb-flavored oil. Cook about 5 minutes, or until wilted.

Add the tomatoes, salt, pepper, and squid. Stir, cover, and cook at a gentle boil for 10 minutes. Uncover and continue cooking for another 10 to 15 minutes, or until the squid is tender. Taste for salt, and add some if desired. Serve with hot, toasted, or fried Italian bread. For 6.

SEPPIE RIPIENE / STUFFED SQUID

2 pounds medium to large squid
2½ salted anchovies, or 5 canned fillets
3 garlic cloves
1 cup loosely packed parsley leaves
2 tablespoons capers
4 tablespoons (approximate) bread crumbs
4 to 5 tablespoons olive oil

1 cup dry white wine
freshly ground pepper

Clean the squid (pages 151–153). If using salted anchovies, fillet them (page 15); if using canned, drain them. Finely chop together the tentacles, anchovies, 1 of the garlic cloves, the parsley, and capers. Put the mixture in a bowl and combine it with the bread crumbs and enough of the oil to make a paste.

Stuff the body of each squid with only a scant teaspoon of stuffing, because in cooking the bodies shrink about one-third of their original size and the filling expands a bit. If overstuffed, the squid ruptures. Once filled, skewer the bodies shut. Save any remaining filling.

Put the rest of the oil into a frying pan large enough to accommodate the squid in one layer. Sauté the remaining 2 garlic cloves in the oil until golden and then discard them. Let the oil cool a moment, and then add the stuffed squid to the pan along with any remaining filling. Cook gently for 8 to 10 minutes. Add the wine, bring to a boil, and cook until the wine has evaporated.

Transfer the squid and sauce to a pan small enough to accommodate the new, shrunken size. Add just enough warm water barely to cover the squid, cover the pan, bring to a gentle boil, and cook 10 minutes. Uncover, taste for salt, and adjust seasonings if necessary, adding a bit of pepper as you please. Boil another 10 minutes, or until the sauce has reduced to half its original volume. Serve warm with the sauce and Italian bread. Stuffed squid are also good as an *antipasto*. For 4.

SOGLIOLONE ALLA ZIA IDA /
FLOUNDER WITH CAPERS

2 tablespoons capers
2 pounds fresh flounder fillets
flour
5 tablespoons butter

1 tablespoon olive oil
3 tablespoons chopped fresh parsley
2 tablespoons fine unseasoned bread crumbs
1½ lemons

Rinse the capers in cold running water, and drain them in a small sieve.

Dredge the fish fillets in flour, patting gently to get as much flour to adhere as possible.

Melt the butter in a large frying pan over low heat, and add the olive oil. Raise the heat and sauté the fish until golden brown on both sides. Remove to a warm platter in a warm place.

Further chop the parsley with the capers, and stir into the melted butter and oil. Add the juice of ½ lemon, sauté 1 or 2 minutes, add the bread crumbs, and stir again.

Spread the fillets with the parsley-caper-butter mixture. Serve with lemon wedges. For 6.

STORIONE IN UMIDO /
STURGEON WITH HERB-AND-TOMATO SAUCE

This elegant way to treat big fish steaks is custom-made for sturgeon, but is also delicious with fresh tuna, swordfish, or other large fish.

2 to 2½ pounds (approximate) sturgeon steak
½ onion
1 celery stalk
1 bay leaf
1½ teaspoons salt, or to taste
freshly ground pepper
2 cups (approximate) dry white wine
2 garlic cloves
3 tablespoons chopped fresh parsley

4 tablespoons olive oil

4 anchovy fillets

2 tablespoons tomato paste, diluted in ⅓ cup warm water, or
3 plum tomatoes, mashed.

If the fish hasn't already been sliced, order steaks cut just about an inch thick. If it's already sliced and thicker than that, just use a dish for marinating which is not so shallow and wide as to leave the fish only partially covered.

Chop together very finely the onion, the celery, and bay leaf. Put this mixture into a deep platter. Place the fish steaks over the herbs. Add salt and pepper and enough wine to cover. Turn the steaks over a few times so that the marinade is well mixed and some of the herbs remain on top of the fish. Let stand for at least 1 hour, turning and basting the fish a couple of times as it marinates.

Finely chop together the garlic and parsley. Put the oil in a saucepan large enough to hold the fish, add the chopped herbs and the anchovy fillets. Cook over low heat for 3 or 4 minutes, stirring slowly, until the anchovies have disintegrated.

Add the fish steaks and cook them on both sides until golden. Add enough of the marinade (strain it if you wish) to cover the fish. Cook for a moment or two. Add the diluted tomato paste or mashed tomatoes. Continue cooking for about 20 minutes or until the fish flesh parts easily when pierced with a fork. Do not overcook. Taste for seasoning during cooking and add more salt to taste if necessary.

Remove the fish to a serving platter and keep warm. Boil the sauce down slightly, pour it over the fish, and serve. For 6.

TONNETTO IN BIANCO / POACHED BONITO

1 4-pound (approximate) bonito

5 parsley sprigs

1 fresh rosemary sprig or 1 teaspoon dried

1 celery stalk with leaves
1 onion, quartered
1 lemon, quartered
6 teaspoons (approximate) salt
10 peppercorns
1 cup wine vinegar
1 recipe *Maionese* (pages 20–21)

Have the fish cleaned but leave the head and tail on. Put it in a fish poacher or the bottom of a roasting pan big enough to accommodate the fish. (If, for lack of space, you must cut off the head and tail, try to fit them in the pan separately to add flavor to the poaching fish.)

Add the herbs, the onion, and the lemon. Pour on the vinegar and enough cold water to cover the fish. Add 1 teaspoon of salt for each quart of water used. Cover the pan, bring it to a boil over medium heat, then lower the heat and simmer 6 minutes to the pound, or until the fish flakes.

Lift the fish out, and skin it while still warm. Then bone it, taking head and tail off as well.

Reassemble the fillets on a serving platter and serve with *maionese*. For 6 to 8.

TONNO FRESCO CON SALSA VERDE /
FRESH TUNA WITH GREEN SAUCE

2½ pounds fresh tuna steak
3 tablespoons vinegar
5 peppercorns
1 bay leaf
½ celery stalk
¼ onion
½ carrot
2 teaspoons salt
1 recipe *Salsa verde* (pages 23–24)

Put the tuna steak in a pan big enough to accommodate it. Add all the other ingredients (with the exception of the *salsa verde*), cover with water, bring to a boil over medium heat, lower the heat, and poach gently for 25 minutes, or until the fish flakes easily.

Remove the fish from the poaching liquid to a serving platter. Cover with half the *salsa verde* and serve. Offer the rest of the *salsa verde* in a separate dish so that it may be added individually, to taste. For 6.

TROTA AFFOGATA / TROUT POACHED IN WINE

3 pounds trout
¼ cup golden seedless raisins, plumped in ½ cup warm water
1 small onion
4 fresh sage leaves
1 garlic clove
1 tablespoon dried rosemary or 2 fresh sprigs
peel of ½ lemon
¼ cup olive oil
⅓ cup wine vinegar
⅓ cup dry white wine
1 teaspoon salt
1 tablespoon (approximate) unbleached all-purpose flour

Clean the trout but leave the heads and tails intact. Rinse well in fresh water.

Finely chop together the onion, sage, garlic, rosemary, and the lemon peel.

Put the olive oil in a big frying pan or saucepan large enough to hold the fish in one layer. Add the chopped herbs and sauté over medium heat until just barely golden. Remove from the heat. Put the fish on top of the herbs. Add the vinegar, wine, and salt. Drain the raisins and add them. Finally, add enough warm water to cover the fish. Bring to a very gentle boil, cover the pan, and simmer about 5 minutes (more or less, depending on the size of the trout), or until the fish are cooked but not falling apart.

Lift the fish from its broth and skin it while it is still warm. Then bone it. Reassemble the fillets on a serving plate and keep warm.

Strain the poaching liquid into a small saucepan. Put the flour into a cup, and spoon in enough of the cooled, strained broth to make a thin paste. Pour the paste into the remaining broth and bring it to a gentle boil, stirring constantly. Boil until the broth has turned into a creamy sauce. Pour on top of the trout and serve immediately, or refrigerate and serve cold. For 4 to 6.

TROTE ALLA GRIGLIA / GRILLED TROUT

4 pounds trout
3 tablespoons chopped fresh parsley
1 teaspoon dried rosemary or 1 fresh sprig
1 garlic clove
1 teaspoon salt
freshly ground pepper
2 lemons
5 to 6 tablespoons olive oil

Start your charcoal grill.

Clean and wash the trout.

Finely chop together the parsley, rosemary, and garlic. Add the salt and pepper (a few twists of the grinder). Mix well and add ½ tablespoon of lemon juice and 1 tablespoon of olive oil, or enough to turn the chopped herbs into a sort of a paste.

Put some of the paste in the cavities of the fish and rub the outsides with the remaining paste. Brush each fish with some of the olive oil.

Grill the trout on both sides over coals, brushing occasionally with olive oil.

Serve with remaining lemon cut into wedges as soon as the fish are cooked.

If a charcoal grill is not available, the trout can be broiled in the oven. Just make sure that the fish sit on a rack so that they won't poach in their own juices. For 4.

TROTELLE ALL'ABRUZZESE /
SMALL TROUT POACHED IN TOMATO SAUCE

4 small trout (½ to ¾ pound each)
2 garlic cloves
6 tablespoons olive oil
3 cups peeled plum tomatoes
5 tablespoons chopped fresh parsley
pinch of oregano
1 teaspoon salt
freshly ground pepper

Clean and wash the trout.

Sauté the garlic in the olive oil in a frying pan large enough to hold the fish comfortably. When the garlic is golden, discard it and let the oil cool a bit.

Put the tomatoes through a sieve or food mill and add to the cooled oil. Cook over medium heat, stirring slowly about 3 minutes, or until the oil and tomatoes have blended together. Add the parsley to the tomatoes. Add the oregano, salt, and pepper (3 or 4 twists of the mill is average). Boil very gently for 10 to 15 minutes, or until the sauce has become thicker and has reduced a bit.

Add the trout to the sauce and simmer covered for 4 minutes. Uncover the pan, turn the fish over, continue cooking at a gentle boil for 4 to 5 more minutes, or until the trout is cooked. Serve immediately.

If you wish, the sauce may be made early in the day, but don't cook the trout until just before serving time. Reheating doesn't do a thing for the fish except spoil them with overcooking. For 4.

TROTELLE CON SALVIA /
BAKED TROUT WITH SAGE

6 small rainbow trout (½ to ¾ pound each)
salt to taste
12 fresh sage leaves
6 tablespoons butter
freshly ground pepper
1½ lemons

Preheat the oven to 450°.

Clean the fish but leave the heads and tails on. Salt the cavities of the fish lightly. Chop 6 of the sage leaves well and sprinkle them inside the fish. Cut 1 tablespoon of the butter into 6 bits and put a bit in each fish.

Butter a baking dish just large enough to hold the fish. Distribute the remaining 6 sage leaves along the bottom. Put in the fish. Sprinkle with salt and a few twists of the pepper mill. Melt the remaining butter and dribble it over the fish.

Bake (at 450°) for 6 to 8 minutes, basting once during baking. Serve with lemon wedges. For 6.

VERDURE / VEGETABLES

If vegetables run the gamut from artichokes to zucchini, so do the many ways (boil to stew) in which they can be cooked. Our modest experience, however, suggests that we pass on to you a word of advice: no matter where or how produced (depending on soil, climate, size, freshness, or individual propensities), the same vegetables tend to cook differently each time. Our weights and timing have worked well for us and are more than rough guidelines; yet the fine details of actual duration of cooking and final seasoning should be suggested (if not dictated) by the vegetables themselves. In other words, do not overcook: a mushy vegetable is a total loss. We test and taste frequently during the cooking and adjust accordingly, and we suggest you do the same. But do not overdo in your tasting: you should leave something to reach the table.

CARCIOFI RIPIENI / STUFFED ARTICHOKES

12 artichokes
juice of two lemons
1 garlic clove
1 tablespoon capers
3 anchovy fillets, canned in oil
1 3½-ounce can Italian tuna
3 tablespoons olive oil

Peel and trim the artichokes (pages 3–7), pry them open with your fingers, and cut out the thistly choke in the very center. Soak the artichokes in water with the lemon juice.

Finely chop the garlic, capers, and anchovies to a paste and mix them with the tuna. Add 1 tablespoon of the olive oil to help bind the mixture.

Drain the artichokes well and fill them with the tuna mixture. Put them stems up in an oven-proof casserole or dutch oven, sprinkle with the remaining olive oil, add just enough water to cover the pot bottom. Cover the casserole and cook for about ½ hour over medium heat, or until the base of the artichoke is tender. During cooking, if the artichokes get a bit dry, add some warm water so that they will not stick. Serve hot. For 6.

CECI E TONNO / CHICK-PEA–AND–TUNA SALAD

1 7-ounce can Italian tuna
2 1-pound cans chick-peas

1 Bermuda onion
2 to 3 celery stalks
4 tablespoons olive oil
salt to taste
freshly ground pepper
2 tablespoons wine vinegar

Drain the tuna, put it in a salad bowl, and break it up with a fork. Drain the chick-peas of the liquid they were canned in and add to the tuna.

Slice the onion into slivers and the celery into very thin slices, discarding the leaves, and add to the salad bowl. Add the olive oil, toss well, add salt, pepper (5 or 6 twists of the mill), and vinegar. Toss well and serve with hot Italian bread. For 6.

CIANFOTTA I /
VEGETABLE STEW, SOUTHERN STYLE

Stew is only barely acceptable as a translation for *cianfotta*. Assorted vegetables congregate together and bask in each other's glory when cooked this way. Almost every Mediterranean country has its own variation, and the following is native to southern Italy.

2 medium eggplants
2 or 3 potatoes (approximately 1 pound)
2 medium zucchini (approximately ¾ pound)
2 sweet peppers (yellow, red, or green)
2 cups fresh peeled plum tomatoes
3 onions
1 celery stalk
¼ cup olive oil
3 or 4 fresh basil leaves
1 teaspoon salt
freshly ground pepper to taste

Wash and prepare the vegetables. First, halve and prepare the eggplants (pages 7–9), and when they have been de-salted, cut them into cubes; peel the potatoes, cut them into small pieces. and soak in water; cut the zucchini into rounds; core the peppers and cut them into strips; cut the tomatoes into small chunks or pass them through a food mill; cut the onions into thin slivers; slice the celery into thin slices.

Sauté the onions and celery in the olive oil in a sizeable pot or dutch oven. When the onions are wilted, add the tomatoes, basil leaves, salt, and pepper.

As soon as the tomatoes start to bubble, add the potatoes and peppers. As soon as the peppers start to wilt, add the eggplants. Cook for 5 minutes and add the zucchini. Cover the pot and boil gently, stirring occasionally, for 20 to 25 minutes, or until all the vegetables are cooked but not turned to a mush. Serve hot or cold. For 6 to 8.

CIANFOTTA II /
VEGETABLE STEW, NORTHERN STYLE

1 small eggplant (optional)
2 onions
1 celery stalk
3 sweet peppers (red, yellow, or green)
3 medium zucchini
2 tablespoons unsalted butter
2 tablespoons olive oil
2 cups fresh peeled plum tomatoes
3 tablespoons chopped fresh parsley
2 teaspoons salt
freshly ground pepper
3 tablespoons wine vinegar

Wash and prepare the vegetables. If using the eggplant, halve and salt (pages 7–9) and after it has drained, de-salt and cut it into cubes. Cut the onions into chunks and the celery into thin slices. Core the peppers and cut them into thin strips. Slice the zucchini into thin rounds.

Melt the butter with the olive oil in a stew pot or dutch oven, and sauté the onions and celery until limp. Cut the tomatoes into small bits and add them to the pot. Add the parsley, salt, and pepper (a few twists of the mill), and bring the mixture to a boil. Add the peppers, and as soon as they start to wilt, add the zucchini. Bring the stew to a boil, add the vinegar, stir well, cover, and cook about 15 minutes. Uncover the pot and cook another 15 minutes, stirring occasionally. Serve warm. For 6 to 8.

INVOLTINI DI MELANZANE /
EGGPLANT-AND-TOMATO CASSEROLE

3 1-pound eggplants (approximate)
salt
flour
vegetable oil for frying
2 garlic cloves
¼ cup chopped fresh parsley
4 large eggs
6 tablespoons bread crumbs
1 cup grated Parmesan cheese
4 cups (approximate) Basic Tomato Sauce (pages 22–23)

Cut the eggplants lengthwise into ½-inch slices and prepare as usual (pages 7–9). After de-salting dip the slices in flour, shake off the excess, and fry them in very hot oil until golden brown on both sides. Drain on paper towels.

Finely chop the garlic with the parsley. Break the eggs into a bowl and mix well with the garlic, parsley, bread crumbs, and about 4 tablespoons of the Parmesan cheese. Add enough water (about 1 tablespoon) to make a spreadable paste. Spread each slice of fried eggplant with the mixture and roll it up.

Preheat the oven to 350°.

With a bit of the tomato sauce cover the bottom of a casserole large enough to hold all the rolled eggplant slices. Make a layer of eggplant rolls, cover with sauce, and sprinkle with some Parmesan cheese. Make a second layer of eggplant rolls, cover with more sauce, and sprinkle with more cheese. Continue layering until all the ingredients are used. Top with a sprinkle of Parmesan cheese.

Bake 25 minutes (at 350°), or until heated through and the cheese has melted into the sauce. Serve cold as an *antipasto* or hot as a second course. For 6.

PEPERONI ALLA CLARA /
CHEESE-FILLED PEPPERS

6 large sweet peppers (red, green, or yellow)
6 tablespoons chopped fresh parsley
½ garlic clove
2 to 3 slices day-old Italian bread
¾ cup (approximate) milk
1 cup grated Parmesan cheese
1 cup *ricotta*
1 teaspoon freshly grated nutmeg
½ teaspoon salt, or to taste
1 large egg
olive oil
1 tablespoon unsalted butter

Preheat the oven to 375°.

Cut off and save the tops of the peppers. Core and seed.

Finely chop together the parsley and garlic. Trim the crusts from the bread, shred it, and moisten it with enough milk to make about 1½ cups of damp bread. Put the bread-milk mixture into a bowl, and add the chopped garlic and parsley, the cheeses, nutmeg, salt, and the egg. Mix well, taste for salt, and add some if desired. Add enough olive oil to make a soft paste.

Fill the peppers with the cheese mixture and dot with butter. Oil the bottom of a baking dish large enough to hold the peppers close together. Put in the filled peppers, cover each one with its own top to keep the stuffing moist during baking, and dribble a little olive oil on each.

Bake for 30 minutes (at 375°), or until the peppers are tender to a fork and the filling has puffed slightly and seems cooked.

Remove and discard the tops. Serve warm as a second course, cold as an *antipasto*. For 6.

POMODORI RIPIENI AL FORNO /
BAKED STUFFED TOMATOES

6 large ripe salad tomatoes
3 eggs
½ teaspoon salt
1½ tablespoons sugar
1 cup unseasoned coarse bread crumbs
½ cup grated Parmesan cheese
grated peel of 1 lemon
¾ teaspoon freshly grated nutmeg
olive oil

Preheat the oven to 375°.

Wash the tomatoes and cut their tops off about ½ inch down, saving the lids. Scoop out the seeds and inner pulp into a sieve. Press out as much juice as you can and save it.

Salt the empty tomato shells very lightly, and turn them upside down to drain on a plate or chopping board.

Beat the eggs in a bowl, and add the salt, sugar, bread crumbs, cheese, lemon peel, and nutmeg. Mix well with a fork. Add enough of the reserved tomato juice (about ¾ cup) to the eggs to make a thick paste.

Fill the tomato shells with the paste and put their tops back on. Put the filled tomatoes in a baking dish just large enough to hold them. Dribble enough olive oil on the tops to make them glisten. Add enough of the remaining tomato juice to cover the bottom of the dish.

Bake (at 375°) for 45 minutes, or until the filling has puffed up and the tomatoes are nicely browned on top. Serve hot or at room temperature. For 6.

SFORMATO DI PATATE /
POTATO-AND-CHEESE SFORMATO

"*Sformato*" is best translated "unmolded," and this dish, assembled as a casserole, is therefore an unmolded casserole. Yet, when ready, it is cut and served as a pie, which it isn't since it has no crust proper. To avoid the whole perplexing issue we will not translate its name at all and will simply call it Potato-and-Cheese *Sformato*.

> 5 eggs
> 6 medium (about 2 pounds) potatoes
> ½ teaspoon salt
> 6 ounces whole-milk *mozzarella* or mild Cheddar, shredded
> 5 parsley sprigs
> 2 fresh basil leaves
> ¾ cup grated Parmesan cheese
> ½ cup unseasoned bread crumbs
> 1 to 2 tablespoons unsalted butter

Preheat the oven to 350°.

Hardboil 2 of the eggs.

Peel and boil the potatoes in salted water to cover. Drain well and mash thoroughly by hand or with an electric beater.

Beat the remaining eggs, add the salt, and mix into the potatoes. Mix the *mozzarella* or Cheddar into the mashed potatoes. Coarsely chop the parsley with the basil and hardboiled eggs, add the Parmesan cheese, and then mix everything into the potatoes.

Butter a 4-quart oven-proof bowl or casserole. Sprinkle in 2 to 3 tablespoons bread crumbs, tilting the bowl back and forth so that the crumbs stick to all sides. Put the mashed, seasoned potatoes into the bowl, sprinkle with the last of the bread crumbs, and dot with butter. Bake (at 350°) for ½ hour.

When the potatoes and cheese have cooled for 10 minutes, run a knife around the edge and unmold onto a serving platter. Serve immediately. For 6.

SFORMATO DI SPINACI /
SPINACH-AND-MUSHROOM SFORMATO

20 ounces fresh spinach, or 2 10-ounce packages frozen chopped
1½ teaspoons salt
1 onion
1 garlic clove
6 tablespoons olive oil
½ cup chopped fresh parsley
½ pound mushrooms
3 large eggs
freshly ground pepper
½ cup grated Parmesan cheese
¾ cup unseasoned bread crumbs

Preheat the oven to 375°.

If using fresh spinach: wash it well, cut off and discard the coarsest stems, and cook with 1 teaspoon of the salt in 1 cup of water in a big pot over high heat. Stir and cook 5 minutes, or until tender. Drain thoroughly in a sieve and, when cool enough to handle, squeeze dry. Chop the spinach coarsely.

If using frozen spinach: put it in a saucepan with 1 cup boiling water and 1 teaspoon of the salt. When tender (about 5 minutes), drain thoroughly in a sieve by pressing the spinach against its sides in order to squeeze out all the water.

Slice the onion into thin slivers, sauté with the whole garlic clove in 4 tablespoons of the olive oil in a large frying pan over medium heat until limp. Remove and discard the garlic when it is golden brown.

Finely chop the parsley, slice the mushrooms, and add both to the onions. Add ¼ teaspoon of the salt, and cook and stir over medium heat for 5 minutes, or until the mushrooms start to get limp.

Mix in the cooked spinach and remove from the heat. Cool a few minutes.

Beat the eggs, add the last ¼ teaspoon of the salt, freshly ground pepper (2 to 3 twists of the mill is average), and the grated Parmesan cheese. Pour the eggs over the spinach and mushrooms and mix well.

Coat the inside of an oven-proof, round, 2-quart bowl or casserole with a tablespoon or so of the olive oil, sprinkle in half the bread crumbs and tilt the dish to make them cling all over the sides and bottom. Add the egg-spinach mixture. Cover with the remaining bread crumbs and dribble the last of the oil over the top. Bake (at 375°) for 15 to 20 minutes, or until the eggs are cooked and the bread crumbs well toasted.

Slip a knife around the edge of the casserole and unmold the *sformato* onto a platter. Serve hot. For 6.

TORTA DI CARCIOFI / ARTICHOKE PIE

FILLING

2 pounds Swiss chard
1 teaspoon salt
6 artichokes
4 tablespoons olive oil
1 onion, finely chopped
freshly ground pepper
2 slices day-old Italian bread
½ cup milk

1 cup grated Parmesan cheese
¼ teaspoon marjoram

CRUST
3¾ cups unbleached all-purpose flour (approximate)
½ teaspoon salt
¼ cup olive oil
1 cup water

Preheat the oven to 350°.

Wash the chard carefully, discarding the toughest stems. Put it in a big pot with a good cover. Cook, using only the water that clings to the chard. Stir as the lower leaves start to wilt, add the salt, put the cover back on, and cook until tender. Drain well in a colander, squeezing the chard against the sides to get out as much water as possible. Chop the chard well.

Prepare the artichokes (pages 3–7) and cut into thin wedges.

Put the olive oil into a large pot, add the onion and artichokes, salt, and pepper, and cook over medium heat until the artichoke wedges are barely wilted. Add the chopped chard, cover, and continue cooking.

Trim the crust from the bread and soak the slices in milk to cover.

When the artichokes are cooked, add the Parmesan cheese and stir well.

Squeeze the milk out of the bread and shred it into the artichoke pot. Add the marjoram, mix well, taste for salt, and add some if needed. Remove from the heat.

Make a mound of the flour, shape into a crater, and put salt, oil, and water in the center. Work with a fork as you would for pasta (pages 52–53), and then knead well until you have a smooth dough.

Break the dough into two parts, one a bit larger than the other. Roll out the larger piece until it seems large enough to cover the bottom and sides of a buttered 10-inch spring-form pan. Line the pan with the rolled dough. Fill with the artichoke-chard mixture.

Roll out the other piece of dough to fit the top of the pan, and cover the pie with it. Pinch the two crusts together. Prick the top with a fork.

Bake (at 350°) for 45 minutes, or until the crust is nicely browned and cooked. Serve hot or cold. For 6.

TORTA DI MELANZANE / EGGPLANT PIE

Fried eggplant slices replace the crust in this open-face pie.

1½ pounds small eggplants (approximate)
vegetable oil for frying
6 eggs
¼ cup milk
½ teaspoon marjoram
2 tablespoons chopped fresh parsley
¼ teaspoon salt
3 tablespoons grated Parmesan cheese

Preheat the oven to 375°.

Cut the eggplants lengthwise into thin slices (¼ inch or less) and prepare as usual (pages 7–9).

In a frying pan bring the vegetable oil to a high heat and fry the eggplant slices until golden brown. Drain on paper towels.

Beat the eggs until foamy, add all the remaining ingredients, and mix well.

Butter an oven-proof casserole (with a capacity of at least 1½ quarts) and line the sides and bottom with the fried eggplant. Pour the beaten egg mixture over the eggplants. Bake 25 to 30 minutes (at 375°), or until the filling has puffed up a bit and is golden on top and cooked through. Serve immediately. For 6.

TORTA DI PATATE E CARCIOFI /
ARTICHOKE CASSEROLE

6 artichokes
juice of 1 lemon
4 medium potatoes
unsalted butter
½ cup unseasoned bread crumbs
3 garlic cloves
¾ cup grated Parmesan cheese
salt
¼ cup olive oil

Preheat the oven to 375°.

Peel and trim the artichokes (pages 3–7). Cut them into thin wedges and drop them in a bowl of water with the lemon juice.

Peel the potatoes, cut them into thin, round slices, and put them in cold water.

Butter an oven-proof casserole, sprinkle in 3 tablespoons of bread crumbs (or enough to coat the entire interior), and turn the dish around and around to get the bread crumbs to cling to the butter.

Fincly chop the garlic and mix it with the Parmesan cheese.

Drain the potatoes and put a layer of them in the bottom of the casserole. Add a layer of artichoke wedges and sprinkle with the Parmesan-garlic mixture. Add a pinch of salt and dribble olive oil over all. Repeat the layering until everything is in the dish. Top with a final sprinkling of cheese, the remaining bread crumbs, and a drop or two more of oil here and there.

Bake (at 375°) for 35 to 45 minutes, or until the potatoes and artichokes are tender to a fork and the bread crumb topping is toasted. For 6.

TORTINO DI VERDURE / VEGETABLE CASSEROLE

    2½ pounds (approximate) assorted vegetables, such as:
        1 medium or 2 small eggplants
        4 tomatoes
        1 big potato
        2 medium zucchini
    ½ to ¾ cup olive oil
    1 cup unseasoned bread crumbs
    4 fresh basil leaves
    3 tablespoons chopped fresh parsley
    1 teaspoon salt
    freshly ground pepper
    3 eggs
    6 ounces whole-milk *mozzarella,* shredded

Preheat the oven to 375°.

Cut the eggplant lengthwise into ½-inch-thick slices. Salt generously and let them stand while you are preparing the rest of the dish. Peel the tomatoes and cut them into wedges. Peel the potatoes and cut them into very thin slices. Take the ends off the zucchini and slice them into thin rounds.

Oil the oven-proof casserole lightly, and sprinkle in enough bread crumbs to coat the inside (about 3 tablespoons).

Chop together the basil and parsley and mix with the rest of the bread crumbs, ½ teaspoon of the salt, a twist or two of pepper.

Beat the eggs well, adding the remaining ½ teaspoon of salt.

To assemble: put all the tomatoes in the bottom of the casserole. Dribble on 2 to 3 tablespoons of the olive oil. Sprinkle with 4 or 5 tablespoons of herbs and bread crumbs. Add about ¼ of the *mozzarella.* Spoon about 3 tablespoons of the beaten egg over the layer.

Make a second layer, using all the potato slices. Sprinkle with the oil, the herbs, bread crumbs, cheese, as before, and spoon on 3 more tablespoons of the egg.

Make a third layer of vegetables using the zucchini slices and proceed as before.

Now scrape the salt off the eggplant slices, pat them dry with paper towel, and arrange as a top layer. Sprinkle with oil, pour on the last of the eggs, and sprinkle with the remaining herbs and bread crumbs.

Bake (at 375°) for 45 minutes. For 6 to 8.

TURTA VERT / RICE-AND-SPINACH CASSEROLE

1½ cups long-grain rice
3¼ cups water
3½ teaspoons salt
8 tablespoons unsalted butter
3 10-ounce packages frozen chopped spinach
1 small onion
4 tablespoons olive oil
6 medium eggs
6 tablespoons grated Parmesan cheese
½ cup (approximate) unseasoned bread crumbs

Preheat the oven to 350°.

Put the rice, water, 2 teaspoons salt, and 2 tablespoons of the butter in a saucepan over high heat. Bring to a boil, stir, cover, lower the heat, and boil gently for 12 to 14 minutes, or until cooked. Stir the rice a couple of times as it boils. Then drain it and run some cold water through it to stop the cooking action.

Cook the frozen spinach in 2 cups of boiling water with 1 teaspoon of the salt until the spinach is completely thawed. Drain thoroughly in a sieve, pressing the spinach against the sides to eliminate all possible water.

Chop the onion and in a large saucepan over medium heat sauté it in 4 tablespoons of the butter and the olive oil until the onion is limp and translucent. Add the drained rice and the chopped spinach and mix well.

Beat the eggs with 3 tablespoons of the Parmesan cheese, add them to the rice and spinach, and mix well.

Butter an oven-proof casserole (a 3-quart round bowl is perfect for this) and sprinkle with 3 tablespoons of the bread crumbs. Turn the casserole around and around to make the bread crumbs cling to the sides and bottom. Fill the casserole with the rice, spinach, and egg mixture. Dot with the remaining butter. Mix the last of the Parmesan cheese with the last of the bread crumbs and sprinkle all over the top.

Bake (at 350°) for 35 minutes, or until the bread crumbs and Parmesan are nicely toasted. For 6 or 8.

ZUCCHINE ALLA MARCHIGIANA /
STUFFED ZUCCHINI

6 medium zucchini
12 parsley sprigs
4 tablespoons unseasoned coarse bread crumbs
4 tablespoons grated Parmesan cheese
½ teaspoon salt, or to taste
¼ teaspoon freshly ground pepper
unsalted butter
4 to 6 tablespoons olive oil

Preheat the oven to 400°.

Wash the zucchini thoroughly and cut off the ends. Cut in half lengthwise and scoop out the inner pulp onto a chopping board.

Chop the parsley leaves and about half the stems with the zucchini pulp. Add 3 tablespoons of the bread crumbs, 2 tablespoons of the Parmesan cheese, the salt and pepper, and mix well.

Fill the zucchini halves with the chopped mixture, patting in the filling gently but firmly. Mix remaining cheese and bread crumbs and pat some on each stuffed zucchini.

Butter an oven-proof casserole that is just large enough to hold the zucchini. Line the halves up in the casserole. Sprinkle with olive oil.

Bake (at 400°) for 30 minutes. Serve either hot or at room temperature. For 6.

ZUCCHINE RIPIENE AL TONNO /
ZUCCHINI STUFFED WITH TUNA

6 medium zucchini (3 to 3½ pounds)
1 7½-ounce can Italian tuna
1 egg
2 tablespoons grated Parmesan cheese
a few drops of Tabasco (optional)
1 teaspoon salt
freshly ground pepper
1 recipe Basic Tomato Sauce (pages 22–23)

Cut off the ends of the zucchini, wash well, and slice into cylinders 2 inches long. Core the pieces and save the pulp.

Put the tuna into a medium-sized bowl, break it up with a fork, and add the egg, the cheese, Tabasco (if you wish), salt, and pepper to taste.

Chop up the reserved pulp and add approximately 1 cup to the tuna mixture, or enough to make a thick paste, and fill the zucchini with it.

Put the stuffed zucchini in an oven-proof casserole (a 10-inch diameter, 3- to 4-quart dutch oven is good), add the tomato sauce, bring to a boil, cover, and simmer 20 minutes, or until the zucchini are tender (yet firm). Serve hot. For 6.

UOVA / EGGS

The egg seems to be the prepackaged foodstuff known to man in all cultures since time immemorial. If there is only one way to crack an egg, there must be a thousand ways to cook it. Italian family techniques are neither many nor sophisticated.

The simplest, perhaps in the belief of leaving well enough alone, is the raw egg technique. We doubt if there is a single boy in Italy who has not been subjected by a loving mother to drinking a fresh egg. A raw egg is said to give stamina, strengthen the muscles, and sharpen the mind. At school exam time, there is traditionally a rush on day-fresh eggs. The method is to crack and remove a portion of the shell and then do your best to drink the egg as from a cup. Sometimes this requires a certain encouragement from Mamma: a well-synchronized slap between the shoulder blades, and down it goes.

Another is *all'ostrica,* the oyster method. Break the egg, remove the white and put the yolk whole into a soup spoon, add a pinch of salt, a pinch of pepper, and a few drops of lemon juice. Imagine it is an oyster and swallow it.

Then come the *uova al tegamino,* two eggs fried in butter or olive oil in small individual earthenware casseroles and served as is, eggs and casseroles both piping hot. Delicious, but be careful with your fingertips.

Then there are *uova in camicia,* or eggs in a shirt (their own); these are poached, really, in salted water or in a tomato sauce.

However, the most common way to serve eggs for more than two is the *frittata,* which can be translated, with some elegance, as the omelet. It is a very simple way to cook eggs, so easy that a description of someone terribly inept is that he or she can't even make a *frittata.*

The basic *frittata* is made with eggs alone, but most frequently it is enlarged and enriched with vegetables. There is hardly an edible herb, green leaf, or tuber that can't go into a *frittata.* The tools are few: a well-seasoned frying pan, skillet, or omelet pan; a fork; a spatula; and a flat plate slightly larger than the pan.

The technique, in general, is this. Prepare and cook the vegetables you will need. Let them cool off a bit. Beat the eggs with a fork until they are really light. Salt them. Mix in the cooled vegetables. Put the pan over medium heat with just enough oil or butter to grease the bottom and sides. The pan should be large enough to accommodate the eggs at a depth of no more than ¾ of an inch (or 1 inch at the most). If the pan at hand is too small for that, cook the *frittata* in two batches. Two small good *frittate* are better than a big bad one.

Once the pan is hot, pour in the egg mixture. Stir the eggs around gently with a fork, making sure the vegetables are evenly distributed. In a minute the bottom solidifies. Go around the edge of the *frittata* with a fork or spatula, and lift it up a little so that some of the uncooked eggs trickle down under. When the top begins to solidify the bottom is, or should be, golden brown. Shake the pan gently back and forth: in a well-seasoned, correctly buttered pan, the *frittata* slides around easily. This is the time to turn it over.

If you are using a pan whose sides are at right angles to the bottom, the plate method is the easiest: place the plate on top of the frying pan, put one hand on the plate, the other on the handle of the pan and turn the two together upside down, letting the *frittata* drop onto the plate, uncooked side down. Then slide it back into the pan. Done, as simple as putting a sleeping baby to bed.

If you have an omelet pan or a frying pan with slanted sides, slide the *frittata* out onto a plate, cooked side down. Turn the pan upside down over the plate, then turn the two together, letting the uncooked side of the omelet hit the pan.

If you are making the *frittata* in two batches (or are cooking only half a recipe — this halves easily), you'll find that slipping a spatula under the omelet is the easiest course. Then lift it up, flip it over and let the uncooked side of the omelet fall back into the pan. Continue cooking until the second side is also golden brown.

A well cooked *frittata* is golden outside, cooked but still moist inside, the vegetables peeking out here and there. Serve hot, cut like a pie. *Frittate* are also served cold as *antipasti.*

FRITTATA AL BASILICO / BASIL OMELET

6 large eggs
3 tablespoons grated Romano cheese
1 cup loosely packed fresh basil leaves
½ teaspoon salt
freshly ground pepper
unsalted butter

Beat the eggs well with 2 tablespoons of the grated cheese.

Chop the basil leaves coarsely and add to the beaten eggs. Add the salt and pepper (a few twists of the mill).

When the omelet pan is hot, put in about ½ teaspoon of butter, or enough to make the bottom glisten. Add the beaten eggs and cook over medium heat until the underside is toasted and cooked solid. Turn it and cook the second side.

When the second side is cooked, sprinkle with the remaining cheese, and serve. For 6.

FRITTATA CON ASPARAGI / ASPARAGUS OMELET

1 10-ounce package frozen cut asparagus
1 teaspoon salt
4 tablespoons olive oil
7 eggs
2 tablespoons grated Parmesan cheese

Thaw the asparagus at room temperature. Pat dry with paper towels.

Heat the olive oil in an omelet or frying pan, add the asparagus and salt, and sauté over medium heat for 5 minutes, or until the stems of the spears are tender to the fork. Cool a moment.

Beat the eggs well, add the cheese now if you wish (or sprinkle the finished omelet with it later), mix well, and pour over the cooked asparagus. Raise the heat, shake the pan back and forth a bit to get the eggs well down and around the asparagus. Cook until the bottom is solid and golden brown. Turn and cook the second side. Sprinkle with Parmesan cheese, if it isn't already in the *frittata*, and serve. For 6.

FRITTATA DI CIPOLLE / ONION OMELET

1½ pounds onions
5 tablespoons olive oil
1 teaspoon salt
freshly ground pepper
½ teaspoon oregano
7 eggs

Cut the onions into thin slivers.

Cook them over a medium-low heat in 4 tablespoons of the olive oil with the salt, pepper, and oregano until thoroughly limp and slightly golden. Let cool for a moment or two.

Beat the eggs well and pour them onto the cooled onion slivers. Mix well.

Heat an omelet or frying pan, add the last tablespoon of olive oil, and then pour in the egg-onion mixture. When the bottom is cooked and golden and the top of the omelet is beginning to solidify, turn the omelet over and cook the second side until golden. Serve warm or cold. For 6.

FRITTATA CON ERBA CIPOLLINA /
CHIVE OMELET

4 tablespoons unsalted butter
7 large eggs
handful of chives, finely chopped
1 teaspoon salt, or to taste
freshly ground pepper

Melt the butter in an omelet pan over low heat. Beat the eggs well.

Raise the heat, put in the beaten eggs, sprinkle with chives and salt and freshly ground pepper. When the bottom is golden brown, turn the omelet and continue cooking. Serve hot as soon as the second side is done. For 6.

FRITTATA CON FAGIOLINI /
OMELET WITH GREEN BEANS

  1 cup water
  1½ teaspoons salt
  1 9-ounce package frozen cut green beans
  4 tablespoons olive oil
  7 eggs

Bring the water to a boil and add 1 teaspoon of the salt and the frozen beans. When the water comes back to a boil and the beans are thoroughly thawed but not completely cooked, drain and pat dry with paper towels.

Heat the olive oil in an omelet or frying pan, add the drained beans, and sauté about 4 minutes, or until tender, turning the beans with a spoon as they cook.

Beat the eggs well, add the last of the salt, and pour the eggs over the cooked beans. Shake the pan to get the eggs well distributed, and when the bottom is solid and golden brown, turn the omelet and cook the other side. Serve hot. For 6.

FRITTATA CON LE PATATE / POTATO OMELET

  1 pound potatoes
  1 small onion
  3 tablespoons unsalted butter
  4 tablespoons olive oil

3 tablespoons chopped fresh parsley
7 eggs
salt
freshly ground pepper

Peel the potatoes and cut them into very small cubes.

Sliver the onion and sauté it in the butter and 3 tablespoons of the olive oil. When the slivers are limp, add the potatoes, salt, and pepper and cook over medium heat until tender. Turn frequently during cooking. Sprinkle with the parsley and then set aside to cool.

Beat the eggs well, add salt to your taste, a bit of freshly ground pepper (3 twists of the mill), and pour over the cooled potatoes. Mix well.

Put the last tablespoon of olive oil in an omelet or well-seasoned frying pan, bring to medium heat, and add the egg-potato mixture. When the underside is golden, turn the omelet and cook the second side. Serve warm or cold. For 6.

FRITTATINE RIPIENE / FILLED ROLLED OMELETS

OMELETS
4 tablespoons flour
4 large eggs
4 tablespoons milk
¼ teaspoon salt
olive oil

FILLING
1 pound fresh Swiss chard or spinach, or 1 10-ounce package
    frozen chopped spinach
4 tablespoons cream cheese
1 tablespoon milk
2 to 3 tablespoons unsalted butter, melted

For the omelets: put the flour in a medium-sized bowl and add the eggs one by one, beating with a fork until all the eggs are in. Mix in the milk, add the salt, and beat again for a moment.

For the filling: if you use fresh chard or spinach, wash it thoroughly, discard the stems, cook in boiling salted water until tender, and drain thoroughly. When the greens are cool enough to handle, squeeze out the last of the water and chop well. If you use frozen spinach, cook it in boiling salted water until tender. Drain thoroughly and squeeze dry as above.

Put the cheese in a medium-sized mixing bowl, add the milk, and mix well with a fork. Add the minced greens and mix again. Taste for salt and add a pinch if needed.

Heat a seasoned omelet pan, add a film of olive oil, and ladle in about ¼ cup of beaten eggs, or enough to make a very thin omelet. Keep the heat of the pan medium-low so that the omelet cooks slowly on the bottom side. When the top looks almost firm, put 2 or 3 tablespoons of filling in the center of the omelet. Roll the omelet up on itself, cook another ½ minute, and remove to a heated plate. Continue making and filling and rolling the omelets until all are done. Dribble with melted butter and serve immediately. Makes 6.

UOVA AL POMODORO /
POACHED EGGS IN TOMATO SAUCE

In Italy, eggs, poached or otherwise, are mostly served for a light lunch or supper. Poaching eggs in tomato sauce is a delicate, tasty way to treat them. This recipe calls for a basil-flavored sauce, but you can substitute Basic Tomato Sauce (pages 22–23) if you don't happen to have any fresh basil.

8 tablespoons unsalted butter
3 cups peeled plum tomatoes
1½ teaspoons salt
10 fresh basil leaves

6 eggs
grated Parmesan cheese, to taste

Melt the butter in a big frying or saucepan. Cut up the plum tomatoes and add them with their juice to the melted butter. Add the salt, stir, and bring to a gentle boil. Cut up the basil leaves coarsely and add them to the tomatoes. Cover, lower the heat, and simmer for 20 to 25 minutes, or until reduced in quantity, thickened, and darkened in color.

When the sauce is ready, add the eggs (as many as will fit comfortably). The eggs will tend to float on the surface, so scoop a spoonful or so of sauce onto the tops of the eggs, and then cover the pan. Cook until the white is firm and the yolk cooked but still soft.

When the eggs are cooked, lift them out with a slotted spoon and put them onto warm plates. Cover with the remaining sauce. Sprinkle with Parmesan cheese to taste and serve. For 6.

CONTORNI

SIDE DISHES

C ONTORNO REALLY MEANS "that which rounds up," but we interpret it freely as "side dish." In an Italian menu that includes meat, the *contorni*, vegetable dishes, are expected to do more than just accompany the main attraction. They are almost as important as the meat itself.

In a meatless menu, however, after a first and second course where vegetables are themselves the stars, a light, delicate salad suffices as an appropriate *contorno*. Thus, in this section, salads lead the list of *contorni*, closely followed by vegetable dishes to be paired with second courses of either fish or *frittate*.

Being extraordinarily fond of salads of all kinds, we are inclined to add one to almost any lunch or dinner. Of course all kinds of fresh greens and vegetables can go into a salad, but the rules for dressing them remain about the same: 2 parts olive oil to 1 part wine vinegar, with salt and pepper to taste. The actual amount of olive oil and vinegar naturally differs according to the amount of greens used, but the relative proportions are unchanged. Also vinegar is sometimes interchangeable with lemon juice.

Boston lettuce (*insalata cappuccina*) should be broken, not cut, into pieces, as should Salad Bowl and American red lettuce. Romaine (*lattuga romana*), curly endive (*indivia*), and escarole (*scarola*) do well when cut: put all the stems together and slice the bunch into 1- to 2-inch lengths. Belgian endive (*insalata belga*) also should be cut with a knife into ½- to 1-inch pieces before it is washed, as its closely fitting leaves do not separate easily for washing before cutting. If, however, the Belgian endive is small, it makes a very pretty salad when cut lengthwise into quarters.

If you have the time, all greens benefit from chilling for ½ hour (wrapped in a clean dish towel or lettuce bag) before being dressed.

INSALATA BELGA / BELGIAN ENDIVE SALAD

    1 to 1½ pounds Belgian endive, cut, washed, and dried
    1 garlic clove
    4 tablespoons olive oil
    salt to taste
    freshly ground pepper
    2 tablespoons wine vinegar

Allow enough time for the prepared endive to chill before assembling the salad (above).

Rub the inside of a salad bowl with a split garlic clove, discarding the clove afterwards.

Put the endive in the bowl, dress with the olive oil, and toss lightly. Add salt and pepper, toss again, and then add the vinegar. Toss lightly once more and serve. For 6.

INSALATA DI CAROTE / NEW CARROT SALAD

    1 pound small new carrots
    2 white celery stalks
    4 tablespoons olive oil
    2 tablespoons lemon juice

1 teaspoon salt
¼ teaspoon freshly ground pepper, or to taste
1 teaspoon sugar
12 Sicilian black olives (packed in brine, not dried)

Cut off the carrot tops and ends. Peel and then cut the carrots into long, thin strips.

Cut the celery into the thinnest slices possible.

Put the two vegetables in a salad bowl, dress with the olive oil, toss lightly, add the lemon juice, salt, pepper, and sugar. Toss well and chill ½ hour before serving. Cut in half and pit the olives; use them to garnish the salad just before serving. For 6.

INSALATA DI CETRIOLI / CUCUMBER SALAD

1 long European cucumber or 3 large American cucumbers
3 teaspoons salt
3 tablespoons olive oil
1½ tablespoons wine vinegar
freshly ground pepper

Peel the cucumber(s) and cut into very thin slices. Put a layer of slices on a platter, sprinkle evenly with salt, and cover with another layer of slices. Salt again, and continue layering until all the cucumber slices and salt are used. Let stand for 1 hour.

Transfer the slices to a colander or large sieve, and rinse off the salt under running water. Spread the cucumbers on paper towels and pat dry.

Put the slices in a salad bowl and dress with the oil and vinegar and abundant pepper. Mix gently. The salad may be served right away, but chilling it for ½ hour improves it. For 6.

INSALATA DI CIPOLLA E ALICI /
ONION-AND-ANCHOVY SALAD

1 pound small onions, cut in thin slivers
6 salted anchovies, or 12 canned fillets
4 tablespoons olive oil
½ teaspoon salt
¼ teaspoon freshly ground pepper
2 tablespoons wine vinegar

Soak the onion slivers in ice-cold water, changing it a couple of times, for at least 3 hours. Drain the slivers and wrap them in 2 or 3 layers of paper toweling to remove as much water as possible before putting them into a salad bowl.

If using salted anchovies, fillet them (page 15); if using canned, drain them. Cut the fillets into 1-inch lengths and add to the onion slivers. Dress with the olive oil, toss, add the salt and pepper, mix well, and add the vinegar. Toss again and serve. For 6.

INSALATA DI FAGIOLI E CIPOLLE /
KIDNEY-BEAN-AND-ONION SALAD

3 pounds fresh kidney beans, or 2 1-pound cans
1 Bermuda or Spanish onion, cut in slivers
4 tablespoons olive oil
freshly ground pepper
2 tablespoons wine vinegar

If using fresh kidney beans, shell them, cook in boiling salted water until tender, and then drain them. If using canned kidney beans, be sure they have been packed in salt and water only, without sugar or sauce of any sort. Drain them in a sieve or colander, and then rinse them off briefly under running warm water to remove any traces of canning liquid.

Soak the onion slivers for 15 minutes in ice-cold water and drain thoroughly.

Put the beans and onions into a salad bowl, add the olive oil, and mix well. Add the pepper and vinegar and mix again. For 6.

INSALATA MISTA / MIXED GREEN SALAD

This simple recipe is included in the hope of convincing 1- or 2-green salad makers that they should diversify and try mixing many greens (and reds) of different flavors and degrees of crunchiness.

¼ head romaine, washed and cut
¼ head curly endive, washed and cut
¼ head red lettuce, washed and broken in pieces
¼ head Bibb lettuce, washed and broken

OR

⅓ head escarole, washed and cut
⅓ head iceberg lettuce, washed and cut
⅓ head Salad Bowl lettuce, washed and broken

AND

2 salad tomatoes (page 10), cut in wedges
¼ red onion, cut in slivers
½ small cucumber, sliced paper thin (optional)
5 tablespoons olive oil
salt to taste
freshly ground pepper
2½ tablespoons wine vinegar

Put the prepared greens and other vegetables into a big salad bowl. Add the olive oil, toss gently, and add the salt and pepper. Toss again and add the vinegar. Mix and serve. For 6 to 8.

INSALATA DI POMODORI / TOMATO SALAD

4 to 6 salad tomatoes (see page 10), cut in thin wedges
5 fresh basil leaves, torn in pieces
4 tablespoons olive oil
salt to taste
½ teaspoon oregano
2 tablespoons wine vinegar

Put the cut-up tomatoes into a salad bowl along with the basil leaves. Dress with the olive oil, toss, add the salt and oregano, and toss again. Add the vinegar, toss, and serve. For 6.

INSALATINA DA TAGLIO CON LA RUGHETTA /
GARDEN LETTUCE WITH ROCKET

This salad, made with the earliest leaves of home-grown salad greens, follows the Italian tradition of using the first of the crop and all of the plant. When you thin the lettuce in your garden, don't throw away the seedlings you've pulled up. Those little 2- to 3-inch leaves of romaine, Salad Bowl, or Bibb are at their sweetest and most tender.

Rocket (in Italian, *rughetta;* also known as roquette or rugola) is a sharp-tasting member of the mustard family whose leaves look rather like a dandelion's. When combined with young lettuce, the two greens bring out the best in each other. But rocket is very different from most herbs used in salads, so we advise you to try a little first: it has been known to divide families into two camps, rocket lovers versus haters. It isn't often found fresh in the American market, but its seeds are available, though you may have to order them from the catalogue of one of the large seed companies. Rocket is very easily grown in the home vegetable patch.

6 handfuls (about ½ pound) new lettuce leaves
5 to 10 rocket leaves

3 tablespoons olive oil
salt to taste
1½ tablespoons wine vinegar
freshly ground pepper

Wash the salad greens and rocket carefully, shake dry, tear into bite-sized pieces, and put into a salad bowl. Dress with the olive oil, toss, add the salt, toss again, and add the vinegar and pepper as for any other salad. For 6.

ASPARAGI AL BURRO E LIMONE /
ASPARAGUS WITH BUTTER AND LEMON

2 pounds fresh asparagus
salt
6 tablespoons unsalted butter
juice of 1 lemon

Prepare the asparagus (page 72) but leave whole, and cook with just enough boiling salted water to cover. When tender but still slightly crisp, remove with tongs and drain on a plate.

Melt the butter in a small saucepan over very low heat. Remove from the heat and stir in the lemon juice.

Transfer the drained asparagus to a hot serving platter and dress with the butter-and-lemon sauce. For 6.

CAROTE AL MARSALA / GLAZED CARROTS

1 pound fresh baby carrots, or 1 20-ounce bag frozen
4 tablespoons unsalted butter
½ teaspoon salt
freshly ground pepper
2 tablespoons sugar
½ cup Marsala wine

If using fresh baby carrots (no longer than 3 inches), peel them and cut in half lengthwise. If using frozen baby carrots, thaw at room temperature.

Sauté the carrots in the butter in a large frying pan for about 6 minutes. Add the salt, a bit of pepper (2 or 3 twists of the mill), and the sugar. Stir and cook another 2 minutes, or until the sugar has melted. Add the Marsala and stir and cook 1 minute. Then cover the pan and continue cooking over low heat for about 5 minutes, or until the carrots are tender. Uncover and cook another 3 to 4 minutes, or until the sauce glazes the carrots. For 6.

CAVOLETTI DI BRUXELLES ALLA BESCIAMELLA / BRUSSELS SPROUTS IN CREAM SAUCE

1½ pounds fresh Brussels sprouts or 1 20-ounce bag frozen
6 tablespoons unsalted butter
2 tablespoons flour
1¼ cups milk
½ teaspoon salt
½ teaspoon freshly grated nutmeg
4 tablespoons grated Parmesan cheese

Cook the Brussels sprouts in boiling salted water until tender and drain thoroughly. Transfer to a flame-proof casserole and dot with 2 tablespoons of the butter.

Put the remaining 4 tablespoons of butter into a saucepan over medium heat, add the flour, and stir until the butter has melted and the flour has been evenly absorbed. Add the milk and continue cooking and stirring for about 5 minutes, or until the sauce has thickened slightly. Add the salt, nutmeg, and 2 tablespoons of the Parmesan cheese.

Pour the cream sauce over the Brussels sprouts. Put the casserole over medium heat and stir gently until all the sprouts are coated with sauce and are hot clear through. Sprinkle on the last of the cheese and serve. For 6.

CAVOLFIORE ALL'AGRO /
CAULIFLOWER WITH OIL AND LEMON

What we are describing here is more a technique than a recipe. All kinds of vegetables besides cauliflower — asparagus, broccoli, green beans, spinach, Swiss chard, and zucchini — are a great treat when prepared this way. There's nothing more to it than simply cooking prepared, cut-up vegetables in boiling salted water until they are *al dente,* tender but still a bit crisp to the bite, and then dressing them with olive oil, salt, pepper, and lemon juice. Dressed this way, all these vegetables are delicious either warm or cool, but not chilled.

1 cauliflower
4 tablespoons olive oil
salt to taste
freshly ground white pepper
juice of 1 lemon

Break off all the flowerets from the main stem or core of the cauliflower. Discard the core and cut the biggest of the flowerets in half. Leave the bite-sized ones whole.

Cook the cauliflower in boiling salted water 8 to 10 minutes or until *al dente.* Drain thoroughly.

Put the cauliflower into a serving dish, add the olive oil, and toss. Sprinkle with some salt and freshly ground white pepper, and add the lemon juice. Toss gently and serve. For 6.

CAVOLFIORE RIPASSATO IN PADELLA /
CAULIFLOWER SAUTÉED WITH ONION

1 large cauliflower
4 tablespoons chopped fresh parsley
1 onion
1 garlic clove

6 tablespoons unsalted butter
1 tablespoon olive oil (optional)
6 tablespoons grated Parmesan cheese

Divide the cauliflower into flowerets, discarding all of the core. Put the flowerets into abundant boiling salted water and cook for 3 minutes after the water comes back to a boil. Drain immediately and set aside.

Further chop the parsley with the onion until they are almost a paste.

Rub the inside of a large frying pan with the garlic and then discard it. Melt the butter in the frying pan, add the chopped onion and parsley, and sauté until golden green. Add the drained cauliflower, stir, and cook for 3 to 4 minutes, or until the flavored butter has coated the flowerets and they have cooked until tender but still crisp. If you wish, add the olive oil at this time.

Sprinkle with the Parmesan cheese, stir well, and serve. For 6.

CAVOLI ALL'AGRODOLCE /
SWEET-AND-SOUR CABBAGE

1 head cabbage (approximately 1½ pounds)
1 medium onion
4 tablespoons olive oil
2 tablespoons tomato paste diluted in ½ cup warm water, or
⅔ cup peeled plum tomatoes and their juice
2 teaspoons salt
2 tablespoons wine vinegar
1½ tablespoons sugar

Take off and discard the rough, outer leaves of the cabbage, cut it into quarters, cut out and discard the core, and slice into very thin strips.

Cut the onion into thin slivers and sauté in the olive oil until limp. Add the diluted tomato paste or, if using plum tomatoes, put them through a food mill or coarse sieve and then add them to the onions.

Bring the tomato-onion mixture to a boil, and add the cabbage and the salt. Cook uncovered, stirring and turning the cabbage, for 2 to 3 minutes, or until the cabbage is limp. Add the vinegar, cover the pan, lower the heat, and cook slowly for 10 minutes. Stir in the sugar and continue cooking covered for about 15 minutes, or until the cabbage is tender but not overcooked. Stir occasionally, taste for seasonings, and adjust if necessary. Serve hot. For 6.

CAZZILLI / SICILIAN POTATO CROQUETTES

2½ pounds potatoes, peeled and cut into chunks
4 tablespoons grated Romano cheese
4 large eggs
½ teaspoon salt, or to taste
2 cups loosely packed fresh parsley leaves, including some
  stems
flour
1 cup (approximate) fine, unseasoned bread crumbs
vegetable oil for frying

Cook the potatoes in boiling salted water until tender. Drain well, mash thoroughly, and continue cooking and stirring over a low heat for about 5 minutes to evaporate as much moisture as possible.

Remove from the heat and stir in the cheese. Let cool a moment. Stir in 2 of the eggs, mixing well. Taste and add salt, as desired. Finely chop the parsley and stir it into the mashed potatoes.

When the mixture is completely cool, flour your hands, and roll the mixture into finger-sized cylinders about 2 to 3 inches long, 1 inch in diameter. Put the rolled *cazzilli* on a plate, but do not stack them. When all of the mixture has been rolled, beat the remaining 2 eggs in a soup plate. Put the bread crumbs into a second soup plate. Dip the *cazzilli* in the beaten eggs and then roll them in the bread crumbs.

Fry the *cazzilli* a few at a time in very hot, deep vegetable oil. When golden brown, remove with a slotted spoon, briefly draining them over the frying pan and then putting them on paper towels to drain further. *Cazzilli* can be served immediately or, if made ahead of time, can be reheated on cookie sheets in a hot oven. When not used as a *contorno*, *cazzilli* are frequently served for a snack. For 6.

CIPOLLE RIPIENE / STUFFED BAKED ONIONS

    3 large (about 2 pounds) Spanish or Bermuda onions
    1 slice day-old Italian bread
    ½ cup milk
    1 egg
    salt to taste
    freshly ground pepper
    6 large mushrooms
    2 tablespoons capers
    1 tablespoon chopped fresh parsley
    1 garlic clove
    ½ cup (approximate) unseasoned bread crumbs
    3 to 4 tablespoons olive oil

Preheat the oven to 375°.

Skin the onions (but do not cut off their tops or bottoms). Boil them for 5 minutes and let cool.

When the onions are cool enough to handle, cut in half horizontally. Scoop out some of the center of each half.

Remove and discard the crust of the bread, and soak the slice in the milk. Then squeeze it almost dry and shred it into a mixing bowl. Add the egg, sprinkle with salt and a few grinds of pepper.

Chop together the mushrooms, capers, parsley, garlic, and some of the scooped-out onion, and add the mixture to the bread and egg. Mash and mix everything well. Fill the onion shells with the mixture. Sprinkle with the bread crumbs.

Put 1½ tablespoons of olive oil in the bottom of a baking dish just large enough to hold the filled onions. Dribble the rest of the olive oil over the stuffing.

Bake (at 375°) for 25 minutes. Serve hot. For 6.

FAGIOLINI AGRODOLCE /
SWEET-AND-SOUR GREEN BEANS

2 9-ounce packages frozen French-cut green beans
1 quart water
1 teaspoon salt
3 egg yolks
3 tablespoons sugar
3 tablespoons wine vinegar
1 tablespoon dry white wine

Thaw the beans at room temperature. Bring the water to a boil, salt it, put in the beans, and cook for 5 minutes or until the beans are tender but still quite crisp. Drain immediately and keep warm.

Put the egg yolks and sugar in a saucepan big enough to hold the beans and beat with a wooden spoon until the sugar has dissolved and the eggs are light in color and fluffy like a cake batter. Stirring constantly, add the vinegar and the wine. Put the pan over a very low heat; cook and stir until the mixture thickens, about 8 minutes. Do not boil.

When the sauce is thick, add the well drained beans and stir and cook 1 minute, or until the beans are heated through and coated with the sauce. Serve immediately. For 6.

FAGIOLINI ALLA PANNA /
GREEN BEANS IN LEMON CREAM SAUCE

1½ pounds fresh small green beans, or 2 9-ounce packages
   frozen French-cut beans
4 tablespoons unsalted butter
¾ cup heavy cream
1 egg
salt
freshly ground pepper
2 tablespoons freshly grated Parmesan cheese
¼ teaspoon freshly grated nutmeg
juice of 1 lemon

If using small fresh beans, cut the stems and tips off, and wash the beans carefully. Cook uncovered in abundant salted water until they no longer taste raw but are still bright green and slightly crisp to the bite. If using frozen beans, you can put them into abundant salted water without thawing and cook them as you would fresh beans. But remember that the frozen ones cook much more quickly. Drain the beans thoroughly and put them into a warm, flame-proof casserole.

Add the butter and stir in all but 2 tablespoons of the cream. Cook over medium heat for a moment.

Break the egg into a small bowl. Add salt and pepper to taste, the remaining 2 tablespoons of cream, the Parmesan cheese, the nutmeg, and the lemon juice. Beat well with a fork until all the ingredients are blended and pour over the green beans. Continue cooking for 2 or 3 minutes, stirring with a wooden spoon until the cream sauce has thickened and coated all the beans. Serve hot from the casserole. For 6.

FAGIOLI ALL'UCCELLETTO /
FRESH SHELL BEANS IN TOMATO SAUCE

This dish is so delicious with fresh beans we hesitate even to mention canned ones. In the interest of those who can't find fresh shell beans, however, we have indicated how to use canned beans, those put up in salted water (no sugar, please).

3 pounds fresh shell beans, or 1½ pounds canned
2 garlic cloves
4 tablespoons olive oil
5 fresh sage leaves
6 or 7 fresh peeled plum tomatoes, or 2 cups canned
1 teaspoon salt

If using all fresh ingredients: shell the beans and put them to boil in abundant, lightly salted water for 15 minutes.

Skewer the garlic cloves with natural wooden picks and sauté them in the olive oil with the sage leaves in a 3- or 4-quart pan until the garlic is golden and the sage limp.

Drain the shell beans and add them to the flavored oil.

Cut the tomatoes in half, remove and discard the seeds, and chop the tomatoes coarsely. Add them to the beans and add salt. Stir well, cover the pan, and simmer for about 20 minutes, or until the beans are cooked. After discarding the garlic cloves, serve.

If using canned beans and tomatoes: drain the beans of their canning liquid and put the tomatoes through a food mill. Flavor the olive oil, as above, add the tomatoes, and simmer about 15 minutes. Add the beans, stir, taste for salt, and add some if necessary. Simmer 5 to 10 minutes and serve. For 6.

FAGIOLONI A CORALLO /
FLAT GREEN BEANS WITH TOMATO SAUCE

1¼ to 1½ pounds flat green beans, or 2 9-ounce packages
  frozen

1 small all-purpose onion, or ¼ Bermuda onion
4 tablespoons olive oil
2 cups peeled plum tomatoes, cut in chunks
1 teaspoon salt, or to taste
¼ cup chopped fresh parsley
freshly ground pepper
salt to taste

If using fresh beans, string them if necessary, remove the ends, wash, and cut into 1½-inch lengths; if using frozen beans, thaw them at room temperature and spread them out on enough paper towels to absorb the excess water.

Sliver the onion and put it into a frying pan with the olive oil. Sauté over medium heat until limp and then add the tomatoes.

Bring the sauce to a boil, add the beans, and return to a boil. Add the salt and pepper to taste. Lower the heat and simmer until the beans are just tender, or about 5 to 10 minutes if frozen, a bit longer if fresh.

Sprinkle with the chopped parsley. Taste for salt, adjust seasonings if necessary, and serve. For 6.

MELANZANE A SCHIBECI /
EGGPLANTS, TOMATOES, AND ONIONS

6 small eggplants
2 medium onions
3 tablespoons olive oil
2 cups peeled plum tomatoes
1 teaspoon salt, or to taste
2 to 3 tablespoons grated Romano cheese

Cut the eggplants in half lengthwise and prepare as usual (pages 7–9).

When the eggplants have wept away their bitter juices, wash them in cold water, dry them on a dish towel, and then cut each half eggplant into thin half-circle slices.

Slice the onions into slivers.

Sauté the eggplants and onions in the olive oil in a medium-sized frying pan over medium heat for about 10 minutes, or until the onions are limp, the eggplant golden. While they are cooking, cut the tomatoes into bite-sized chunks. Then push the semicooked vegetables to one side, add the tomatoes on the other side, and cook 10 minutes, or until the tomatoes have started to disintegrate. Mix all three together, add the salt, lower the heat, and cook another 10 minutes. Sprinkle with the Romano cheese and serve. For 6.

PADELLATA DI VERDURE / MIXED VEGETABLES

2 large onions, cut in chunks
2 medium (about 1 pound) eggplants, salted, drained, and cubed (pages 7–9)
1 carrot, sliced paper thin
1 small head of curly endive, cut in chunks
2 sweet peppers (about 1 pound), roasted and cut into strips (page 36)
½ teaspoon salt
1½ teaspoons marjoram or oregano
¼ cup vinegar

Sauté the onions in the olive oil over medium heat in a large saucepan or dutch oven. When barely wilted, add the eggplants and the carrot. Cook, stirring frequently, until the eggplants begin to wilt. Then add the endive, the peppers, salt, and marjoram (or oregano). If during cooking the vegetables do not add enough natural juices to keep them moist, add 1 or 2 tablespoons of warm water. Continue cooking until the endive stems are tender.

Stir well, add the vinegar, cover the pan for about 1 minute, or until the vinegar stops sizzling, and then uncover and continue cooking for another 2 or 3 minutes. Serve hot or at room temperature. For 6 to 8.

PATATE A TOCCHI /
POTATOES SAUTÉED WITH ONIONS

1½ pounds potatoes
1 onion
4 tablespoons olive oil
4 tablespoons unsalted butter
1½ teaspoons salt, or to taste
3 tablespoons finely chopped fresh parsley

Peel the potatoes and cut them into small, irregular chunks (*tocchi*).

Cut the onion into very thin slivers and sauté in the olive oil and butter. When the onion slivers are limp, add the potatoes and salt and cook over medium heat, turning frequently with a spatula, until tender.

Add the parsley and stir and cook a moment longer. Serve hot. For 6.

PEPERONATA / SWEET PEPPERS WITH TOMATOES

6 (about 2 pounds) sweet peppers (red, green, and yellow)
¼ cup olive oil
2 large onions, cut in chunks
½ teaspoon salt
¼ cup wine vinegar
3 large salad tomatoes, cut in chunks

Core and seed the peppers and cut them into chunks.

Put the olive oil in a large saucepan, add the peppers, the onions, and the salt. Cook and stir over medium heat about 10 minutes, or until the peppers and onions are limp.

Add the vinegar, cover the pan, and cook for 1 minute.

Uncover the pan, add the tomatoes, stir well, and continue cooking 20 to 25 minutes, or until the natural juices of the vegetables have reduced and thickened, the tomatoes have disintegrated, and the peppers are cooked and tender. For 6 to 8.

PISELLINI AL BURRO / PEAS WITH BUTTER SAUCE

1 large onion
2 garlic cloves
8 tablespoons unsalted butter
2 10-ounce packages frozen tiny peas, thawed
2 teaspoons oregano
½ cup dry white wine or water

Cut the onion into very thin slivers and skewer the garlic on a wooden pick. Sauté the onion and garlic together in 4 tablespoons of the butter until the onion slivers are limp.

Add the thawed peas and the oregano, stir well, and add the wine (or water). Cover, and cook over low heat for 10 minutes. Uncover, add the remaining 4 tablespoons of butter, and cook and stir until the butter is melted. Remove and discard the garlic. Serve hot. For 6.

PISELLINI ALL'OLIO / PEAS WITH OLIVE OIL

2 pounds fresh tiny peas, or 2 10-ounce packages frozen
1 Bermuda onion
⅓ cup olive oil
1½ teaspoons salt
freshly ground pepper
½ teaspoon sugar

If using frozen peas, thaw at room temperature.

Peel the onion and slice into thin slivers. Sauté the onion in the olive oil in a large frying pan or saucepan until slightly golden, limp, and translucent.

Add the peas to the onions. Add the salt, pepper, and the sugar.

Cover and continue cooking about 5 to 7 minutes, or until the peas are tender. Serve hot. For 6.

RAPE BIANCHE / WHITE TURNIPS

   1½ to 2 pounds small white turnips
   3 quarts water
   3 teaspoons salt
   2 garlic cloves
   3 tablespoons olive oil
   3 tablespoons chopped fresh parsley
   freshly ground pepper
   2 tablespoons chopped turnip greens (optional)

Peel the turnips, washing and saving the leafy tops (if any), and cut into wedges.

Cook the cut-up turnips in the boiling salted water 10 minutes, or until just tender. Drain well.

Sauté the garlic in the olive oil in a large frying pan until golden and then discard the cloves. Add the drained turnips, the chopped parsley, and abundant pepper. If your turnips come with greens, chop the tops and add to the turnips with the parsley. Sauté over high heat 5 to 10 minutes, or until the turnip wedges are lightly browned around the edges. Serve hot. For 6.

SPINACI AL POMODORO /
SPINACH WITH TOMATOES

   10 ounces fresh spinach
   2 teaspoons salt
   4 tablespoons olive oil
   2 garlic cloves
   2 cups peeled plum tomatoes, cut in chunks
   freshly ground pepper

Wash the spinach thoroughly, discarding the toughest stems. Cook in a big, covered pot using only the water that clings to the leaves. Add 1 teaspoon of the salt and stir the spinach as it cooks. Remove the pot from the heat the minute the spinach is limp. Drain well and, when cool enough to handle, squeeze out all the remaining water.

Sauté the garlic in the olive oil in a large saucepan until golden and then discard the cloves. Let the oil cool a moment. Add the tomatoes, the other teaspoon of salt, abundant pepper, bring to a boil, and then lower the heat. Simmer 15 minutes.

Add the drained spinach, stir well, raise the heat, and cook another 5 minutes. For 6.

SPINACI COLL'UVETTA / SPINACH WITH RAISINS

1¼ to 1½ pounds fresh spinach
1½ teaspoons salt
⅓ cup golden seedless raisins
3 tablespoons unsalted butter
2 tablespoons olive oil
2 garlic cloves
2 to 3 tablespoons pine nuts (optional)

Cut off and discard the thickest spinach stems. Wash the leaves thoroughly, and put them into a big pot. Add the salt, cover, and cook in the water that clings to the leaves. Stir a couple of times during cooking. Remove the pot from the heat when the spinach looks very limp but is still a bit crisp to the bite.

Drain well in a colander, squeezing out as much water as you can by pressing the spinach against the sides with a big spoon.

Soak the raisins in ½ cup of warm water. Melt the butter with the olive oil in a large frying pan. Add the garlic cloves, sauté until golden, and then discard them. Add the drained spinach and continue cooking 5 minutes, stirring frequently. Drain the raisins, pat them dry with a paper towel, and add to the spinach. (Stir in the pine nuts now, if you are using them.) Cook and stir 1 more minute, and serve. For 6.

DOLCI

DESSERTS

D OLCI, ITALIAN SWEETS, can be divided into two classes: the deliciously monumental creations of ceremonial affairs and the simpler concoctions for family feasts. Both sorts come from a long tradition.

One cannot think of the first class without visualizing the sweet, sculptured, daring constructions of the ducal *Mastri Pasticceri*, master pastry cooks, and their platoons of assistants. Today, city pastry shops, open weekdays and Sundays, duplicate in good measure the ancient royal art, perfuming the air with sugar and spice. Whole families take Sunday trips to a *pasticceria* to choose which *dolce* will please the three generations, all agonizing over the selection of one or two favorites, a hard choice when the whole shop is filled with sweets to charm even the most anti-dessert member of the group. These same shops, on weekdays, furnish another but simpler *dolce*, the sweet buns enjoyed with a morning coffee on the way to work or school.

When it comes to family *dolci*, our thoughts race back in time to all the Christmases, New Years, Easters, birthdays, name days, saint's days, homecomings, leave-takings, exam passings, holiday openings and holiday closings, or any other reason for celebrating. The aroma of those family sweets rose and fell with the draft from an opening door, mingled with the faint fresh smell of table linen dried in the sun and of flowers brought to the lady of the house, be she mother, grandmother, aunt, or cousin.

Those sweets also carry with them the memory of a festive day when every village family, rich or poor, would bring their *dolci* to be baked in the baker's communal, wood-fired brick oven. On those days, the fragrance of baking bread would mix with that of the sweets and fill the air. It is impossible to say if the church bells rang more for the joy of that fragrance or to the glory of the saint of the day.

The recipes included here are not only some of those we have used for our celebrations but also some which have been offered to us in country kitchens by generous people whose welcome never seemed to flag and whose goodbyes included many a package of cookies thrust into our hands as a token of friendship or Godspeed when we took to the road.

Of course, make them all. Some go together quickly, others take more time, but they are all very authentic. They belong to a type of dessert that is fast disappearing. We think they are gastronomic treasures. Historically, they have no part in the *cucina di magro*. But they all traditionally appeared on the Italian table right after the fasting was over. Surely, the time is now.

ANICINI / ANISE BISCUITS

6 eggs, separated
1 cup sugar
1½ cups unbleached all-purpose flour
1½ teaspoons baking powder
pinch of salt
2 tablespoons anise seeds

Preheat the oven to 350°.

Beat the egg yolks with all but 2 tablespoons of the sugar until pale yellow in color and the consistency of frosting.

Sift the flour with the baking powder and salt into the eggs a bit at a time, mixing well after each addition. Add the anise seeds and mix again.

Beat the egg whites with the remaining 2 tablespoons of sugar until stiff, and then fold into the egg yolk mixture.

Butter two 5″ x 10″ loaf baking pans, and put half the dough into each. Bake (at 350°) 45 minutes to an hour, or until a cake tester comes out dry.

Remove from the oven, and cool slightly before removing the loaves from their pans. Slice each loaf into ½-inch-wide slices. Place on cookie sheets and return to the oven. Turn the slices over when top sides are toasty brown, and remove when both sides are done.

BISCOTTINI PIEMONTESI / SUGAR COOKIES

These cookies are very similar to many of the butter cookies made in America but differ in the flour used: more than half is corn flour, the very finest ground cornmeal which is available in Italian groceries and many American supermarkets where Mexican and Puerto Rican produce is sold. This finest ground cornmeal is the same texture as ordinary unbleached all-purpose flour. It is also used for *Zaleti* (see page 251).

    2 cups finest corn flour
    1⅔ cup unbleached all-purpose flour
    1¼ cups sugar
    pinch of salt
    3 large eggs (at room temperature)
    ½ pound unsalted butter, softened
    1 teaspoon vanilla, or grated peel of 1 lemon

Preheat the oven to 375°.

Sift the two flours together with the sugar and salt onto a pastry board or counter. Form a crater and put the eggs and the butter in the center. Stir and work the eggs and butter as you would to make pasta (pages 52–53), and add the vanilla or lemon peel. When you have a well-amalgamated dough, roll it into a ball, wrap in wax paper, and let it sit for ½ hour or so.

Attach a star tube or opening to your pastry bag or cookie press and fill with dough. Press out strips about 4 inches long onto floured cookie sheets.

Bake (at 375°) for 10 minutes, or until golden. Makes about 70 cookies.

BOCCONOTTI / FILLED SUGAR COOKIES

FILLING
½ cup apricot or peach jam
1 ounce unsweetened baking chocolate, grated
2 tablespoons citron, chopped
juice of ½ small lemon
2 tablespoons rum
½ teaspoon vanilla
2 teaspoons finely ground coffee

DOUGH
1 cup lard
1 cup sugar
4 egg yolks
3 cups (approximate) unbleached all-purpose flour

unsalted butter
unseasoned bread crumbs

Preheat the oven to 350°.

In a small bowl mix together the jam, chocolate, citron, lemon juice, rum, vanilla, and coffee. (The jam should be the lumpy kind, with real pieces of fruit in it; and if you don't have a coffee grinder or blender that will pulverize beans into a powder, crush drip grind coffee with a rolling pin or heavy glass.)

Cream the lard and sugar together until you have an even-textured blend. Add the egg yolks, one at a time, mixing well after each yolk is added. Sift 2½ cups of the flour into the mixture a little at a time and mix well.

When all the flour has been used, you should have a soft, rather moist dough. Flour the counter, the rolling pin, and your hands with the remaining flour. Work the dough briefly with your hands and cut it in half. Roll out each piece of dough into a sheet about ⅛ inch thick. Cut into rounds about 2 inches in diameter.

Butter the cookie sheets, sprinkle them well with the bread crumbs, shake them, and discard the crumbs that don't adhere.

Using a spatula, lift half of the discs off the counter and put them on the cookie sheets.

Put 1 teaspoon of filling on each disc and cover with remaining discs. Crimp around the edges with fingers or fork to seal in the filling.

Bake 20 minutes (at 350°), or until light brown. Makes about 2 dozen.

BUDINO DI RICOTTA / RICOTTA PUDDING

⅔ cup toasted slivered almonds
5 eggs
1 pound *ricotta*
½ cup confectioners' sugar
grated peel of 1 lemon
unsalted butter
¼ cup unseasoned bread crumbs

Preheat the oven to 375°.

Crush the almonds in a mortar or blender until reduced to fine bits. Place in a small bowl, add 1 egg white, and mix well.

Beat the *ricotta* in a large bowl with an egg beater or stir it well with a fork to make it light and fluffy. Mix the almonds and egg white into the *ricotta*.

Beat the yolk and the remaining eggs and the sugar well and fold into the *ricotta* mixture. Add the lemon peel and mix well.

Generously butter a 2-quart ring mold or Bundt pan and sprinkle with the bread crumbs, turning and tilting the pan to make the crumbs adhere evenly on the bottom, sides, and center tube.

Pour the *ricotta* mixture into the pan, distributing it evenly with the back of a spoon or spatula.

Bake (at 375°) for 1 hour, or until puffed up, golden on top, and a cake tester comes out clean. Let it cool in the pan, and then turn it out onto a serving platter. For 8.

CASSATA SICILIANA / SICILIAN CASSATA

CAKE

5 large eggs (at room temperature), separated
1½ cups sugar
¼ teaspoon salt
1½ cups unbleached all-purpose flour
¼ teaspoon cream of tartar
1 teaspoon vanilla
½ teaspoon grated lemon peel

FILLING

½ pound *ricotta*
⅔ cup heavy cream
1 packet unflavored gelatin
¾ cup light or dark rum
⅔ cup sugar
2 ounces sweet baking chocolate, grated
1 tablespoon candied citron, slivered
8 candied cherries, quartered
¼ cup sliced pistachios or almonds

1 recipe *Zucchero glassato* (page 234)

Preheat the oven to 350°.

Separate the eggs into two 2½-quart bowls. Beat the yolks, add the sugar, and keep on beating until pale yellow and the consistency of frosting. Beat the whites until stiff, adding the salt as you beat. Gently fold the whites into the yolks, being careful to turn the batter over and over, going all the way down to the bottom of the bowl and around the edges.

Sift the flour and cream of tartar together three times, and fold it into the eggs slowly. Fold in the vanilla and the grated lemon peel.

Butter and flour a 10″ x 6¼″ rectangular cake pan. Pour in the batter and bake (at 350°) for 30 minutes, or until a cake tester comes out clean. Cool before cutting.

While the cake is cooling, you can make the filling:

Beat the *ricotta* 1 minute with an egg beater.

Beat the cream in another bowl until stiff, and then fold it into the *ricotta*.

Moisten the gelatin with 4 tablespoons of the rum, and then warm over low heat for 3 minutes or until dissolved. Cool a moment.

Fold the gelatin-rum mixture into the *ricotta* and cream. Fold in the remaining ingredients, one at a time.

When the cake is cool, turn it out onto a bread board and cut it in ¼-inch slices.

Now you are ready to begin the mold. Using a 2-quart bowl, line its bottom with slices of the cake and place more slices around the sides vertically. Dribble rum on each of the slices. Spoon half the filling into the bowl, on top of the rum-soaked bottom slices. Cover with additional pieces of cake and then add the rest of the filling. Cover with the remaining slices of cake. If any of those standing vertically come up above the top of the *cassata*, cut them off and use them also on the top. Dribble with the remaining rum.

Dribble *zucchero glassato* (caramel sugar) back and forth to cover, more or less, each exposed piece of cake, but be careful not to let the sugar go down any cracks around the side of the bowl (which would result in a large piece of tooth-cracking caramel). Chill at least 4 hours.

When the *cassata* is chilled and ready to be served, turn it out sugar-side down on a serving platter. Cut with a very sharp knife. For 10 to 12.

ZUCCHERO GLASSATO / CARAMEL SUGAR

  1 cup sugar
  2 tablespoons water
  pinch of cream of tartar

Put the sugar in a small saucepan with the water and cream of tartar. Mix well, cook over low heat at first, and then raise it to medium. Stir from time to time, and when the sugar has reached a temperature of 300° (the hard-crack stage), remove it from the heat and use as directed, but quickly, before it hardens.

CENCI / TATTERS

Cenci can be reasonably translated as tatters. They are Florentine sweets, cut into strips which are further cut to tatters. Traditionally made for the last day of *Carnevale*, Mardi Gras, *cenci* are winners with the small fry at any time.

  2 tablespoons unsalted butter, softened
  ½ cup (approximate) confectioners' sugar
  1 tablespoon brandy, cognac, or *grappa*
  2 eggs
  pinch of salt
  2 cups unbleached all-purpose flour
  vegetable oil for frying

Make a dough as you would for pasta (pages 52–53) by putting the butter, 2 tablespoons of the sugar, the brandy (or cognac or *grappa*), 2 eggs, and salt in the center of a well of flour. Mix it with fork and hands until smooth. Roll it into a ball, cover it with a clean kitchen towel or piece of plastic wrap, and let it rest for ½ hour.

Roll out the dough with a rolling pin or a pasta machine until it is very thin (the thickness of a dime). Using a pastry cutter, cut the dough into strips 2½″ x 4½″.

Make four lengthwise slits in the middle of each strip, stopping short ½ inch from both top and bottom. Next, take the three strands of dough on the left of the strip and slide them through the remaining slit on the right hand side. Then take one end of the now almost braided dough and slide it through any possible opening. Your lovely pastry now looks like a rather hopeless bundle. Continue cutting, slipping through, and twisting until all are completed.

Bring the frying oil to 350°, hot enough to make a bit of dough sizzle when dropped in. Fry a few *cenci* at a time, and watch them blow up quickly in odd contorted shapes. Turn when golden brown on one side, remove when golden on both sides. Place the *cenci* on absorbent paper, and sprinkle with the remaining sugar. Delicious served with a sparkling wine.

CIAMBELLA DELLA NONNA /
GRANDMOTHER'S CAKE

1½ cups sugar
¾ pound less 3 tablespoons unsalted butter
3 large eggs (at room temperature), separated
¾ cup potato flour
1 cup unbleached all-purpose flour
2 teaspoons baking powder
½ teaspoon salt
1 teaspoon vanilla

Preheat the oven to 325°.

Cream the sugar and butter together until very soft and pale in color. Beat the egg yolks well and add them to the sugar and butter, mixing in thoroughly. Sift the two flours and the baking powder together, and add a little at a time to the egg mixture.

Beat the egg whites until stiff, adding the salt as you beat. Fold the egg whites into the yolks and sugar. Fold in the vanilla.

The dough is very thick, almost like cookie dough, and should be dropped by the spoonful into a buttered ring pan, smoothing off the top of the dough with the back of the spoon or a spatula once it is all in the pan.

Bake (at 325°) for 45 minutes to an hour, or until the cake has risen and is a golden, crusty brown on top. Do not open the oven during the first 35 minutes of baking. Test with a cake tester or thin skewer before removing from the oven. If the tester emerges clean, the cake is ready. Cool before cutting. For 10 to 12.

CIAMBELLONE / RING CAKE

¾ cup golden seedless raisins or ½ cup raisins plus ¼ cup
   candied citron
7 tablespoons lightly salted butter
1 whole egg plus 2 egg yolks
⅓ cup sugar
2 cups unbleached all-purpose flour
4 teaspoons baking powder
½ teaspoon salt
1 cup milk
grated peel of 1 lemon
confectioners' sugar

Preheat the oven to 350°.

Soak the raisins in a cup of warm water to soften them.

Put the butter in a pyrex mixing bowl over a pan of warm water over medium heat until the butter is melted. Cool for a few minutes. Add the sugar, whole egg and egg yolks. Beat with an electric mixer for 3 minutes, or until the eggs and sugar have blended well.

Sift the flour twice, add the baking powder and salt, and then sift once more directly into the egg mixture, adding a little at a time alternately with the milk as you continue beating at the lowest speed. Add the grated lemon peel. Beat for 15 minutes after all the flour and milk are in. Remove the beaters, scraping off as much dough as you can.

Drain the raisins, and squeeze them dry in a paper towel. Add the raisins to the dough.

Butter a spongecake or angel food cake (tube) pan and dust with 2 tablespoons of mixed flour and confectioners' sugar. Toss out that which doesn't cling to the sides and bottom.

Spoon the dough into the pan. Bake for approximately an hour, or until golden brown on the top (which cracks as the cake rises) and a cake tester comes out clean. Sprinkle with confectioners' sugar as it cools in its pan. When cool, turn out on a plate and cut as you wish. For 10 to 12.

CREMA DI LIMONE / LEMON CREAM

½ pint heavy whipping cream
¼ cup sugar
1 lemon
⅓ cup light rum

Using a hand-held or stationary mixer, whip the cream, starting at low speed and working up to high. When the cream is almost completely stiff, whip in the sugar at low speed. Grate the lemon peel and add it to the cream, still using low speed. Squeeze ½ lemon, strain the juice, and beat it into the cream. Whip in the rum.

Fill 6 dessert or custard cups with the lemon cream. Chill thoroughly in the freezer but for no more than 1 hour. For 6.

CROSTATA DI FICHI / FRESH FIG PIE

DOUGH
2 cups unbleached all-purpose flour
1 cup sugar
10 tablespoons unsalted butter, softened
3 egg yolks
grated peel of 1 lemon
pinch of salt
1 egg white

FILLING
10 to 12 fresh ripe figs (green or purple)
½ cup confectioners' sugar

Preheat the oven to 350°.

Make a mound of the flour on the counter or pastry board, hollow out a well in the center and put the sugar, butter, egg yolks, lemon peel, and salt into it.

Mix as you would pasta (see pages 52–53), stirring the center with a fork, breaking the eggs, collecting flour and sugar. Keep on stirring until it becomes too difficult to work with a fork, and then work with your fingers to amalgamate everything and make a smooth dough. Roll it into a ball and cover with a clean dish towel or napkin or put into a plastic bag. Chill for ½ hour.

When it is thoroughly chilled, break off about a third of the dough and put it aside for a lattice topping. Roll out the remaining dough to fit the bottom and part way up the sides of a 10-inch spring-form or a *quiche* pan. Put the rolled dough into the pan, pushing it with your fingers to fit into the edges.

Peel the figs and cut them into quarters or sixths, depending on the size of the figs, and arrange over the bottom crust, covering it well. Sprinkle the figs with confectioners' sugar.

Roll out the remaining dough and cut it into strips with a pastry cutter. Place the strips lattice-fashion over the figs, pinching the ends of the strips together with the lower crust where they meet.

If any dough is left over, run it around the edge to make a border.

Beat 1 egg white lightly and paint the strips and border. Bake (at 350°) for ½ hour. Cool before serving. For 8.

GELU DI MELONE / WATERMELON JELL

1 4- to 5-pound watermelon
4 tablespoons cornstarch
1 cup sugar
½ teaspoon vanilla
1 ounce unsweetened baking chocolate
cinnamon

Put the pulp of the watermelon through a sieve or food mill to make 4 cups of melon juice.

Put the melon juice into a 3-quart saucepan, add the cornstarch, sugar, and vanilla, and bring to a boil. Stir and boil until the juice has thickened and coats the spoon.

Grate the chocolate and stir it into the still boiling juice. When the chocolate has blended into the juice, remove the pan from the heat, cool a bit, and then pour into custard cups.

Chill well and serve with a sprinkling of cinnamon. For 10 to 12.

BISCOTTO DI SAVONA / SAVONA CAKE

5 large eggs (at room temperature), separated
1 cup sugar
⅓ cup plus 1 tablespoon potato flour
½ cup unbleached all-purpose flour
grated peel of 1 lemon
pinch of salt
¼ teaspoon lemon extract
confectioners' sugar

Preheat the oven to 350°.

Separate the eggs into two large bowls. Beat the yolks for 30 seconds, add the sugar, and continue beating until the mixture is very thick and very pale in color.

Sift the flours together and gradually fold into the egg yolk mixture, a little at a time, making sure that all the flour has been completely absorbed before you add more. Fold in the grated lemon peel.

Beat the egg whites until stiff, adding salt as you beat. Fold the egg whites into the yolks and flour. Fold in the lemon extract.

Butter and flour a Bundt pan and pour in the cake batter. Bake (at 350°) for 45 minutes. Cool upside down on a cake rack.

Remove the cake from the pan, and put it, bottom side up, on a serving platter. Sift 2 or 3 tablespoons of confectioners' sugar through a fine sieve directly onto the cake. For 8 to 10.

PANE GAJARDO / FRIED BREAD

12 ¾-inch slices day-old Italian bread
5 medium eggs
olive oil
jam, or confectioners' sugar to taste

Beat the eggs well in a shallow bowl. Dip in the slices of bread one by one, turning quickly to coat both sides with egg. Remove to a frying pan containing just enough hot oil to cover the bottom. Fry the egg-dipped bread to a golden brown on one side, and then turn and fry the other side.

Serve as a snack immediately with the jam of your choice, or with a simple dusting of confectioners' sugar. For 6.

PASTA FRITTA / FRIED PASTA WITH HONEY

This dish is said to be the most hygienic dessert served by the people of Syracuse; it's said to give strength to rich and poor alike in times of joy or famine.

> 1 pound *capelli d'angelo* (*vermicelli* of the finest sort)
> 5 quarts water
> 5 teaspoons salt
> oil for frying
> 6 to 8 tablespoons natural dark honey

Bring the water to a boil, salt it, add the *capelli d'angelo* by the handful, stirring so that they don't stick together. Cook over medium heat. The minute the pasta has reached the *al dente* stage, plunge a long fork into the pan, turning as if to eat from the pan, and extract, one by one, six forksful of *capelli* all wound-up. Place each bundle of drained pasta on a plate to cool. (This can be done hours ahead of serving time if you wish.)

Deep fry the cooled, wound-up pasta in hot oil until crisp and golden and then remove and drain well. Put a forkful of fried pasta in each of 6 dessert bowls or plates.

Heat the honey and add a tablespoon or so to each little nest of pasta. For 6.

PERE AL VINO / PEARS BAKED IN WINE

> 6 Bosc or Seckel pears
> 2 cups (approximate) dry red wine (Burgundy, Chianti, or Barolo)
> ½ cup sugar
> 6 whole cloves

Preheat the oven to 400°.
Wash the pears, but do not peel them or remove their stems.

Put them into a baking dish just large enough to hold them, stems up. Pour the wine over the pears up to ¾ inch from their tops. Sprinkle with sugar, and add the cloves.

Bake (at 400°) for 1 hour, or until the pears are tender.

Lift the pears out of the baking dish into a serving bowl. Pour the remaining wine into a saucepan and boil it down until almost syrupy. Pour it over the cooling pears and serve, or cool completely before serving. For 6.

PERE RIPIENE / STUFFED BAKED PEARS

    6 Bartlett pears
    ¾ cup crushed almonds and walnuts
    6 tablespoons sugar
    1 egg
    unsalted butter
    1½ cups (approximate) dry white wine

Preheat the oven to 400°.

Peel the pears, halve them, and remove and discard their cores. Scoop out a bit of pear from each center and reserve.

Mash the nuts to a paste, using either a mortar and pestle, a blender, or a rolling pin.

Chop up the reserved pear bits and mix with the nuts and 4 tablespoons of the sugar. Stir in the egg. Fill the pears with the nut mixture.

Generously butter a baking dish just large enough to hold the 12 pear halves. Put the pears in the dish (if any of them tilt too much, slice off a bit of the pear to make them sit properly) and dribble the wine over the pears and into the bottom of the pan to a depth of at least ¾ inch. Sprinkle with the remaining 2 tablespoons sugar.

Bake (at 400°) for 45 minutes, or until the pears are tender. Add a bit more wine if the dish gets dried out before the pears are cooked. For 6.

PESCHE AL VINO / PEACHES IN WHITE WINE

6 firm ripe peaches
2 tablespoons sugar
dry white wine

Wash the peaches and thinly slice them directly into a serving bowl. Sprinkle with sugar and pour over enough white wine to cover. Turn the peaches to distribute the sugar. Chill for at least ½ hour before serving. For 6.

PIZZA DOLCE / SWEET PIZZA

DOUGH
1 cake fresh yeast
⅓ cup warm water
3 cups (approximate) unbleached all-purpose flour
4 large eggs
¼ cup sugar
5 tablespoons vegetable oil
¼ teaspoon salt
1 teaspoon vanilla

FILLING
¼ cup seedless raisins
1½ squares unsweetened baking chocolate
¼ cup chopped walnuts
¾ cup toasted, slivered almonds
¼ cup pine nuts
¼ cup candied citron
3 large eggs
½ cup sugar

Dissolve the yeast in the warm water, stirring it carefully to make sure that it really is dissolved.

Make a mound of the flour on the counter, turning it into a crater. Add the yeast water and stir it in with a fork, going around and around the crater as you would for pasta (pages 52–53), collecting flour as you stir. Add the eggs, stir some more, and when all the eggs are well absorbed, sprinkle in the sugar. Finally, add the oil, 1 tablespoon at a time, the salt, and the vanilla.

When the dough becomes too difficult to mix with a fork, flour your hands and work the dough with your fingers until it is smooth and soft and has absorbed all or most of the flour. Form a ball and put it in a bowl, cover the bowl with a plate, and let the dough sit for ½ hour in a warm place until it has risen to at least half again its original size.

While the dough is rising, prepare the filling: plump the raisins up by soaking them in a cup of warm water. Chop together the chocolate, nuts, and citron. Beat the eggs and set aside a tablespoon or so for painting the crust. Add the sugar. Drain and pat dry the raisins and add them to the beaten eggs. Add the chopped chocolate, nuts, and citron. Mix well.

Preheat the oven to 350°.

Flour the counter. Mold the dough with your hands into a sausage shape and cut off a quarter of it and set aside. Using a floured rolling pin, roll out the larger piece of dough so that it will fit the bottom of a baking pan 10 inches in diameter and come up the sides about 1½ inches. A spring-form pan is fine for this. The dough is very elastic and will resist its climb up the sides, but by pushing it and manipulating it with your fingers this bottom crust of the pizza will stay put.

Pour the filling into the bottom crust.

Roll out the other piece of dough to fit on top of the filling. Tuck in the edge of the lower crust underneath the edge of the upper crust. Press lightly with your fingers to get the two crusts to stick together. Go around the edges a second time, pressing with a fork.

Brush the top of the pizza with that tablespoon of reserved beaten egg. Make tiny holes in the crust with a cake tester, skewer, or fork to let the pizza breathe as it bakes.

Bake (at 350°) for 45 minutes to 1 hour, or until golden brown on top and puffed up, when a cake tester stuck in near the edge of the pizza (away from the moist center) will come out clean.

Cool thoroughly before removing from the pan and before serving. For 12.

TORTA DI FRUTTA / FRUIT PIE

This is a dessert to fit any month of the year, any region of the country. It uses fresh fruit when available, dried figs when the market can't provide something seasonal. Each fruit has its own spice or flavoring, and the whole thing goes together simply, especially with two pairs of hands, one for the dough and one for the fruit and spice.

FRUIT
Any *one* of the following:
   4 apples
   6 peaches
   3 cups blueberries
   3 cups sliced strawberries
   5 pears
   12 ounces dried, soft figs
juice of 1 lemon

DOUGH
10 tablespoons unsalted butter, softened
¾ cup sugar
4 eggs
2 teaspoons baking powder
½ teaspoon salt
2 cups unbleached all-purpose flour
flavoring:
   1 teaspoon vanilla for apples or pears
   1 teaspoon almond extract for peaches or figs
   1 teaspoon lemon extract for blueberries or strawberries

SUGAR AND SPICE FOR FRUIT AND DOUGH
cinnamon and nutmeg for sprinkling on apples
extra sugar for sprinkling on all fruits except figs
confectioners' sugar for sprinkling on top crust

TO PREPARE THE FRUIT

Apples: peel and core, cut them into very thin slices, put them in a bowl, and sprinkle with the juice of 1 lemon. Turn the slices over and over to dampen well with the lemon juice in order to prevent browning.

Peaches: don't peel; cut them into halves, discard the stones, cut into very thin slices directly into a bowl, and mix well with the lemon juice.

Blueberries: wash them well, discarding any stems that may cling to the berries. Turn out to dry a bit on absorbent paper, and then mix them with the lemon juice in a bowl.

Strawberries: wash them well, hull, slice, put them in a bowl with the lemon juice, and stir.

Pears: peel and core them, cut into thin slices, and mix in a bowl with the lemon juice.

Figs: remove the stems from the figs (use the soft, sticky ones, not the hard, very dried kind), and cut each fig into 4 or 5 pieces.

TO PREPARE THE DOUGH

Cream the butter and sugar well with a fork. Add the eggs, one at a time, mixing well after each addition. Beat with an electric mixer until light in color, fluffy in texture, and until the sugar no longer grates against the side of the bowl. Sift the baking powder and salt with the flour and add it, sifting for the second time, bit by bit to the eggs and sugar, mixing well after each addition. The dough by this time has almost the consistency of drop-cookie dough. Mix in whichever flavoring suits the fruit you are using.

TO ASSEMBLE THE PIE

Preheat the oven to 350°.

Butter a 9-inch spring-form pan. Drop spoonfuls of dough into it and spread them with a rubber spatula to get a layer about ½ inch thick.

If using apples: spread a layer and sprinkle with cinnamon and a bit of sugar. Add another layer and sprinkle with nutmeg and sugar. Use the last of the apples for the third layer and sprinkle with sugar.

If using peaches, blueberries, strawberries, or pears: make three layers, sprinkling each with sugar only.

If using figs: make one layer.

Drop the remaining dough by the spoonful and spread it as smoothly as possible with the spatula. (It spreads awkwardly but do the best you can, the heat of the oven will complete the spreading where you can't.) Bake (at 350°) for 45 minutes. Sprinkle with confectioners' sugar as it cools, and serve cool.

TORTA DI MELE / APPLE CAKE

1 lemon
2 pounds baking apples (Cortland, Spy, Baldwin)
½ cup (approximate) sugar
2 large eggs (at room temperature), separated
1 cup unbleached all-purpose flour
¼ teaspoon salt
1 teaspoon baking powder
¾ cup milk

Preheat the oven to 350°.

Grate the lemon peel and reserve it. Squeeze the lemon itself, straining the juice into a large bowl.

Peel and core the apples and cut them into thin slices directly into the bowl with the lemon juice. Add 2 tablespoons of the sugar and toss well so that all the slices are moistened with the juice.

Separate the eggs. Beat the yolks with 2 more tablespoons of the sugar for 3 minutes, or until the sugar has dissolved and the yolks are pale yellow, the mixture the consistency of boiled frosting.

Sift and mix the flour, salt, and baking powder into the eggs a little at a time, alternating with tablespoons of milk until all the flour is used. Mix and add the remaining milk. Stir in the grated lemon peel.

Beat the egg whites until stiff, and fold them into the dough.

Fold in the apple slices.

Bake (at 350°) in a buttered 9-inch cake pan (a spring-form pan is ideal for this) for ¾ hour, or until the seemingly meager amount of dough has puffed up and the top of the cake is toasted. Sprinkle with the remaining sugar. Cool before serving. For 8.

TORTA DI ZIA RITA / FILLED PASTRY RING

CRUST

2 cups unbleached all-purpose flour
2 tablespoons sugar
⅛ teaspoon cinnamon
⅛ teaspoon salt
1 large egg (at room temperature)
3 tablespoons vegetable oil
6 tablespoons dark rum or Marsala wine

FILLING

5 tablespoons honey
5 tablespoons rum
grated peel of 1 lemon
2 heaping tablespoons cocoa
½ teaspoon cinnamon
1 tablespoon sugar
1 cup finely chopped walnuts
½ cup slivered almonds, chopped
4 tablespoons damson plum jam

⅓ cup unseasoned bread crumbs, toasted in 1½ tablespoons
   unsalted butter
milk

Sift the dry ingredients for the crust onto a pastry board or
counter, make a hollow in the center, and add the egg, oil, and
about half the rum. Mix as you would pasta (pages 52–53), adding the last of the rum after the other liquids have been blended
in. Work with your hands until the dough is uniform and smooth.
Wrap it in plastic and put it in the refrigerator to chill for ½ hour.
   Preheat the oven to 350°.
   While the dough is chilling and the oven heating, make the
filling. Put the honey in a small saucepan over low heat. Add
the rum and stir and heat until the honey has dissolved.
   Remove the pan from the heat and stir in all the other filling
ingredients (except the bread crumbs and butter), mixing well
after the addition of each one. In a small frying pan toast the
crumbs in the butter until brown. Now stir them into the filling.
   When dough has chilled, flour your counter or use a pastry
cloth and roll out the dough to the thinnest possible rectangular
sheet. If you don't have a pastry cloth, try a knitted rolling pin
cover, which aids in making this somewhat stiff dough roll out
smoothly.
   With a spatula spread the filling over the entire surface of the
crust, leaving only ½ inch bare at the edges. Roll the crust up on
itself as you would a jelly roll.
   Generously butter a medium-sized ring pan and curve the roll
of filled pastry around the ring. Bring the two ends together,
slipping one inside the other, and secure with 2 or 3 wooden picks
so that the filling won't run out. Brush the top lightly with milk.
   Bake (at 350°) for 30 minutes, or until the crust is browned on
top. Cool in the pan, and then turn out onto a serving platter.
For 8.

TORTA DI ZUCCA GIALLA / PUMPKIN PIE

This is a versatile Venetian pie which uses either pumpkin or squash, fresh or frozen. It's good the day it's cooked, better the day after, and it can be frozen for serving weeks later.

CRUST

¾ cup unbleached all-purpose flour
1 tablespoon unsalted butter, softened
pinch of salt
¼ cup (approximate) water

FILLING

2 pounds fresh pumpkin or Hubbard squash, or 2 12-ounce
   packages frozen cooked squash
1 or 2 cups milk, depending on the type of pumpkin used
⅔ cup toasted, slivered almonds
½ cup (approximate) sugar
1½ teaspoons cinnamon
pinch of salt
3 eggs

If using raw, fresh pumpkin or squash: peel it, cut it into chunks, and boil it in 2 cups of milk until tender. Put the cooked pumpkin pieces in a cheesecloth-lined sieve, and press out as much liquid as possible, which should leave you approximately 2 cups of pumpkin with which to work.

If using frozen, cooked squash: thaw at room temperature, put it into a cheesecloth-lined sieve, and squeeze out the excess moisture, giving you 2 cups of pureed squash.

Put the pumpkin (or squash) into a large mixing bowl. Crush ⅓ cup of the almonds in a mortar or blender, and add to the pumpkin along with the sugar, cinnamon, and a pinch of salt. Stir in the eggs one at a time, and mix well. Add 1 cup of milk to the pumpkin mixture if you used the frozen type. Taste for sugar and adjust accordingly.

Preheat the oven to 350°.

Make the crust as you would pasta (pages 52–53), and roll it out into a very thin disc large enough to cover the bottom and go up the sides of an 11-inch pie pan.

Fill the crust with the pumpkin mixture. Sprinkle with the remaining slivered almonds. Bake (at 350°) for 45 minutes, or until the pumpkin mixture is firm and does not stick to a knife when inserted. For 6 or 8.

ZALETI / CORNMEAL PATTY CAKES

⅔ cup golden and dark raisins, mixed
½ pound unsalted butter
⅔ cup sugar
3 egg yolks
1½ cups finest corn flour
1½ cups unbleached all-purpose flour
½ teaspoon salt
1 teaspoon baking powder
grated peel of 1 lemon
confectioners' sugar.

Preheat the oven to 350°.

Plump the raisins up by soaking in 2 cups warm water.

Cream together the butter and sugar. Beat the egg yolks and add them to the butter mixture. Sift the corn flour and all-purpose flour with the salt and baking powder and add to the eggs and butter a little at a time, mixing well after each addition.

Drain the raisins, pat them dry with paper towels, and stir them into the dough along with the grated lemon peel.

Flour your hands and the counter. Work the dough briefly, press it down, and shape it gently into a roll about 2 inches in diameter. Cut the roll into slices about ½ inch thick and press them into rounded ovals.

Put the *zaleti* on buttered cookie sheets and bake (at 350°) for 20 minutes, or until slightly puffed up and golden. When baked, sprinkle with powdered sugar and cool. Makes 2½ to 3 dozen.

INDEX